THE MAGIC OF MATSUMOTO:

THE SUZUKI METHOD OF EDUCATION

BY

CAROLYN M. BARRETT, Ph.D.

Library of Congress Cataloging-in-Publication Data

Barrett, Carolyn M., 1941-
    The magic of Matsumoto : the Suzuki method of
education / by Carolyn M. Barrett.
        p.   cm.
    Includes bibliographical references (p. 143).
    ISBN 0-88280-126-0
    1. Music—Instruction and study—Juvenile. 2. Suzuki,
Shin'ichi, 1898- . I. Title.
    MT1.B325 1995
    780'.7—dc20   94-39778
                                      CIP
                                     MN

Published by ETC Publications
       700 East Vereda del Sur
       Palm Springs, CA 92262-4816

Published in the United States of America.

To my granddaughter, Mariam, who taught me once again the innocence,
joy and creativity of childhood.

TABLE OF CONTENTS

Suzuki Method
Talent Education Institute
Shinichi Suzuki
President & Director

3-10-3 Fukashi, Matsumoto-shi
Nagano-ken 390   Japan
Tel:0263-32-7171

I believe that this book will deepen the understanding of the Suzuki philosophy and movement and will be of help to parents and for the worldwide movement for all children's happiness.

Shinichi Suzuki

ACKNOWLEDGMENTS

To Dr. Shinichi Suzuki for encouraging me and believing in me.

To Ernestine Ducheneaux and her husband Frank who lent moral support and helped with the early preparation of the manuscript.

To Sania Hussain who took on the task of word processing and cheerfully handled continual changes.

To my English 302 students whose courage and integrity inspired me.

To my music students who kept me going through it all.

To my daughter Tracey who was my first "Twinkler."

To Faiyaz Haider who challenged me and who saw the manuscript through to camera ready condition.

INTRODUCTION

It was a fine sunny October day in Matsumoto, Japan. As I began the walk from my hotel to the Talent Education Institute to finish the research for this book (feeling not a little inferior to the task), I was surprised to see Toba Sensei speed by on her motor bike. She stopped to greet me. At least I knew someone in this city of strangers.

Toba Sensei was a Suzuki student who had completed the Suzuki program before it became well known in the United States, and who had been selected by Dr. Suzuki to go to Oberlin to share the Suzuki Method and pursue her own studies. She had transferred to Fort Wright College in Spokane, Washington, where she studied with Sister Xavier Mary Courvoisier (a Juilliard graduate), and where a successful Suzuki program had been established.

It had been in Spokane in 1968 ten years previously that I had first met Toba Sensei and at Fort Wright that I had had my first introduction to the Suzuki Method. I, too, was studying with Sister Xavier Mary and my two-and-one-half-year-old daughter, Tracey, had been interested in learning the same thing Mommy was learning.

So here was Toba Sensei almost ten years later. Talking with her reminded me that I had forgotten the bottle of Napoleon Cognac I had brought on the plane for Dr. Suzuki. Toba Sensei had told me, when I called from Seoul to be sure

Dr. Suzuki would be in Matsumoto when I arrived, that he was celebrating his birthday on the seventeenth. He must be nearly eighty. Back to the hotel for the brandy and again the walk to the Institute.

I had a strange emotional reaction like that of coming home as I walked up the steps of the Institute. I had been here in the wilting heat of August and the freezing cold of January. It was nice to be here in the crisp but not chill coolness of October. This was my third visit. I had struggled with the violin here, although I hadn't brought my violin this time; this was to be a writing trip. I had struggled with teaching here. Perhaps I had struggled with myself here. Perhaps that was why it seemed like home. Or was it because there were others here, even Dr. Suzuki, who had struggled with the same things and who shared and encouraged others in their own struggle?

As I walked into the foyer of the Institute, I saw a gentleman lost in study at the shelf displaying books on Dr. Suzuki and the Suzuki Method. Anxious to see if something new had been written since I last visited, I began my own perusal.

To my surprise, Dr. Himo Kim, head of the Ta Institute in Korea, came around the corner. We were very surprised to find each other in Matsumoto. Our last contact had been in May of 1977 when we combined our students to present the first All Korea Suzuki Concert. Fifty-five children on stage played from Books One through Five. It had been quite an occasion.

Dr. Kim had helped me find a Korean Suzuki teacher to take my students so I could concentrate on my studies for this book; he told me that he was in Matsumoto to observe the kindergarten education program run by Dr. Suzuki. We proceeded to the office together, where we learned Dr. Suzuki was giving a television interview but would be with us when he finished.

Dr. Suzuki's ideas were being applied to developing pre-school (schooling usually starts in Korea and Japan at the age of seven) and kindergarten programs. Dr. Kim was very interested in doing this and, in fact, had established a kindergarten in Seoul and one in Cheong-Ju in Korea. He now wanted to establish what he translates into English as a "Lane Kindergarten" in Cheong-Ju. This would benefit the children of the very poor and would be free of charge. There would be no classrooms, no teaching instruments, just learning in the lanes, which is where these children spend most of their time anyway. The innovative nature of such a program would be tremendous. Dr. Suzuki's success in teaching the violin to the very young gives enough credence to the idea to make it a possibly imminent development in Korea and Japan.

While we waited to see Dr. Suzuki, we were escorted to the kindergarten room to observe what was happening there. I couldn't help but reflect on the waves of change that are radiating from Matsumoto—change not only in violin pedagogy but also in the very structure of education in Korea and Japan. The class was being conducted in Japanese. There was one Western child in the room and we could not fail to notice each other. Dr. Kim was very excited with the teaching that was underway and translated for me. What we saw was not the stereotyped rigid authoritarian atmosphere so often associated with Oriental classrooms.

Time came for art instruction and Dr. Kim reacted with excitement as the teacher began eliciting from the students what they would like to draw. Again, this was a change from the usual authoritarian pattern. These will be far-reaching changes if they are indeed implemented throughout Japan and Korea.

Then came word that Dr. Suzuki was now teaching. Would we like to join him?

It was like coming home to return again to his studio. He recognized and greeted us with his own special warmth and seemed quite happy to have two teachers from the Korean Suzuki movement in his studio.

Dr. Suzuki was working with Japanese kenkyusei, or teacher trainees, this morning and resumed teaching. The first translation into English he chose to make followed a student performance of a portion of a Vivaldi concerto. "Music must come from the heart, not the liver," he exclaimed. This he followed with a demonstration of the sound he wanted to hear and some technical advice on how to produce it. "Watch the speed of the bow. Use crescendo and decrescendo."

The students laughed with him at the comparison of heart and liver, then concentrated mightily on producing the sought-after-sound. Dr. Suzuki seemed lost in thought for a moment, then said:

This is my leisure. If I am exhausted, teaching revives me. I do not scold. We enjoy together, then they can learn. It all goes back to the mother tongue method. Does a mother scold her child when it first says "Mama" and say, 'No hold your lips this way. Say mmm, not mm."No. Never scold."

Here to me seemed to be the heart of his teaching. There is a great regard and concern for the student. There is no assumption that the student is stubborn, recalcitrant, or lazy. There is an assumption that the student is trying as best he or she can to learn and the teacher must be there, helping. Scolding and threatening are not helpful. There is a striking parallel here to Carl Rogers' concepts of student-centered teaching which will be discussed more fully in Chapter Five.

When the morning's lessons were finished, I presented Dr. Suzuki with the Napoleon Cognac, which he accepted enthusiastically. In the ensuing warmth, I dared to ask him questions that seemed audacious, yet I felt I needed to have his answers.

"What is art?" I asked.

"Art is ability. It is potential. It is the potential of every human being. It is the expression of self. Art can be the Tchaikovsky Violin Concerto, or it can be a discussion between two human beings. It is communication of self from one to another."

"What then is ability?"

"Living soul makes ability and every human being has the capacity to have and express living soul. Ability is not in heredity. Everyone has the capacity for various kinds of virtuosity. Environment shapes ability."

"Why is music important if discussion between two human beings, communication, is the same as art?"

"Before communication takes place there must be feeling or the possibility of empathy. It is this feeling, this capacity for empathy that is taught through music. It is possible to communicate with Mozart and Bach if one has this capacity for empathy.

"Music is the best medium for educating the whole human being. In learning language or becoming expert at mathematics, feeling is not developed. The entire human being, especially his emotions, must be educated to a very high level in order for there to be civilization. Now civilization is at a very low level. It is stone age in level. Everything is decided by militarism. Perhaps in 500 years there will be some progress. I will come back then to see; you must come back, too, and Dr. Kim. Civilization now is a 'mistake'."

"But how can it happen?" I questioned, "One machine gun can kill us all with one burst of the trigger."

"Only start," replied Dr. Suzuki. "Thirty years ago there was nothing in Matsumoto. No music. I had six students. Now it is full of music. I have hundreds of students in Matsumoto. I have students in the Berlin Philharmonic, students teaching in Canada and in the United States. Only begin to develop the emotions to a high level and it will continue."

Then, strangely enough, Dr. Suzuki began talking about the control of anger. "This, too, is a part of the Suzuki Method," he said. "The ability for anger is not a good ability. It must not be developed," he insisted. "I decided to lose the ability for anger. The first year was the most difficult year."

"That would be harder than learning to play the violin," was my response.

"The first year I had many bad feelings in my stomach," Dr. Suzuki said. "But after ten years, I no longer have the ability. I cannot get angry."

The parallel between what Dr. Suzuki described about anger and operant conditioning or, in this case, de-conditioning, seems incredible. Would it be possible to condition the human race away from the ability to become enraged? No one would pull the trigger of that ubiquitous machine gun or push the nuclear button? A fantastic concept. Yet, Dr. Suzuki claims to have done it for himself. Astonishing, but when I think of the permeation I see of Dr. Suzuki's teaching with operant conditioning (discussed in Chapter Two), it is perhaps not so impossible. The application of Dr. Suzuki's method of teaching the violin to dealing with an emotional problem that besets the human race at an increasing pace seems almost plausible.

But how did he do it? That is the next question. And that is the intriguing question about his violin method. How does he do it? How does he help little ones to learn so well? Indeed, how does he help everyone to learn so well, because the method works with learners of all ages and backgrounds. My book is an attempt to find the answers. How *does* the "Magic of Matsumoto" actually work?

I see many modern theories used by educationists at work in the Suzuki Method: operant conditioning, total use of technology, use of modeling behavior, programmed instruction, student-centered teaching, mastery learning. These different components function together to create an amazingly effective way of teaching. The effectiveness can be seen in the skills created: six-year-olds playing Vivaldi's Concerto in A Minor and playing it well; four-year-olds playing a Bach Bourrée; ten-year-olds playing two Mozart concertos and in command of a large performing repertoire. How does this happen?

My answer is that, in addition to the Western theories mentioned above, an abundance of theory often only suggested in the West is actually being put to use in the Suzuki Method also. Students are expected to perform all suggested exercises and behaviors. This, in combination with centuries-old traditions of "teaching and learning," produce a very powerful instruction method. The final ingredient is a spiritual (not religious) component that permeates all and is "first cause" as well as final ingredient.

WESTERN STUDENTS IN MATSUMOTO

When I returned to Dr. Suzuki's studio after a Japanese lunch of cold noodles, it was filled with twelve foreign students. These were young violinists and teachers from the United States and New Zealand. I remember similar sessions from other Matsumoto visits where other foreign faces (Australian, English, American) appeared, and was suddenly struck with wonder: what brings foreigners from distant lands to this tiny city in western Japan to study the violin? One young American man said he was convinced the Suzuki approach was *the* very best method for introducing students to the violin. After earning his M.A. in violin and studying with various concert violinists, he had considered the option of the Eastman School of Music but had decided on coming to Matsumoto for two years. One reason was the Suzuki bowing technique. It is unique and is taught by Dr. Suzuki in much the same way that archery is described as being taught by a Zen master in *Zen in*

7

the Art of Archery. It is something you simply have to experience.

There are other similarities to Zen in Dr. Suzuki's teaching (discussed in Chapter Eight), not the least of which are his pithy maxims. These convey clearly to the student the necessity for a certain technique—"poor intonation is like a cup of coffee with salt in it"—if not the means to attaining the required technique.

More difficult and even more Zen-like are such sayings as "good tone is tone with living soul." The extraordinary haunting vibrancy of Dr. Suzuki's tone on the violin makes one agree. But how does one go about producing tone with living soul? Dr. Suzuki's advanced students have such a tone and it is not a replica of the Master's tone. It is their own living soul in the tone, yet the quality is so characteristic that one could almost call it "Matsumoto Tone," as we speak of Matsumoto Tempo. Dr. Suzuki suggestively speaks of international intonation (a comment that brings a smile but also makes an emphatic impression on the foreign student).

But what is it really that brings these students to Matsumoto? I thought of the cut-throat competition in many music schools—the drive to accomplish, outdo, achieve. I thought of the pressure, the loneliness, the isolation. Here, each student is cherished and nurtured with profound respect. There is no belittling, nor any overblown congratulating. It is a difficult task that is being undertaken and effort is required and respected. Achievement is fairly estimated. Each student's struggle is honored. No one is considered less talented nor of less worth in the eyes of the Master. Each student's struggle is held in great esteem. Although the techniques of virtuosity may be readily available from many sources in their native country, the nurturing of each student's self is not likely to be equally available. While many universities espouse the development of the whole human being, they seem to go about it in a very piecemeal sort of way. Each department educates its bit of the student and somehow he or she is supposed to have put the educated bits together on graduation day.

Here in Matsumoto, Dr. Suzuki educates not bits but the whole person. Bowing technique, left-hand technique, are not separate entities. They must work together through the brain to allow the soul to express itself in living tone.

It is not always pleasant and easy. Western students have told me that the first few months in Matsumoto are sometimes very difficult indeed; "ego-shattering" was the word. This is particularly true of the accomplished violinist who is accustomed to overwhelming and impressing with his/her achievements. The bow technique usually provides the most difficulty and Dr. Suzuki spends hours working patiently with such students. He devises new approaches for each student—playing the entire first section of the trio of Beethoven's Minuet in G in one up bow was a device I saw him use on this day. It is difficult for students to work diligently on such maneuvers when they can perhaps play the Mendelssohn violin concerto smashingly. Yet, it is very clear that the sound is not "right" and they must keep trying. Dr. Suzuki uses a whole-arm technique that is quite challenging to achieve for everyone, especially those who have had their bowing fragmented into individual wrist, elbow, finger, and shoulder movements.

Repeated and again-repeated efforts ("Practice that 10,000 times," says Dr. Suzuki) are necessary to learn this difficult technique, yet the notes are simple. It looks simple when Dr. Suzuki does it. It is simple, but not easy. The newcomer is apt to be overwhelmed with the simplicity of it all, and wonder why others seem to have such difficulty. The tenth time the student is told to practice "Twinkle" 10,000 times, using the whole-arm technique, he or she begins to realize Dr. Suzuki is after something very particular and that he intends to achieve it. He is firm and kind, but unrelenting. There is a real process of deconditioning and reconditioning going on here, but

9

it is far from Pavlovian or Skinnerian conditioning. It is humane conditioning. The oft-repeated Matsumoto dictum, "Violin is easy; music is difficult," doesn't help much; but the kindness, respect, and concern of the Master do. That is what sustains the students through to mastery. That is the real heart of the difference in the Suzuki Method.

Yet, every great teacher has respect, concern and kindness for students. This essential humanity is linked to a battery of fine pedagogical techniques: humane conditioning; the use of every possible device of modern technology to assist in the struggle; a program of instruction; a curriculum that has been painstakingly selected, revised, reviewed; the use of modeling behavior to cross the gap between technical instruction and intuitive doing. The power of this combination cannot be overestimated and is concretely validated by the amazing achievements of Dr. Suzuki's violinists.

CHAPTER 1

BIOGRAPHY AND HISTORY

Dr. Shinichi Suzuki was born in 1898 in Nagoya, Japan, the son of the founder of Japan's largest violin factory. His father, Masakichi Suzuki, had first become experienced in the art of constructing musical instruments through the family side-line of the construction of samisens, a banjo-like instrument. This was a supplementary business for a poor samurai and had been begun in the days of Masakichi's grandfather.

Born in 1859, Masakichi eventually went to Tokyo to become an English-language teacher. His desire to become a teacher of English seems quite a remarkable thing to have occurred in Japan in the 1800s. He must have been a person with considerable progressive spirit. Perhaps there is a foreshadowing here of the internationalism and independence of spirit that would animate his son, Shinichi.

In the 16th Century, an ancestor of the violin, the viol, was played by Christian missionaries in Japan before Prince Oda. After the persecution and oppression of Christians by the Tokugowas, the sound of the violin was not heard again until the 1800s, when people became fond of it.

Masakichi became interested in Western musical instruments and began step-by-step research into the violin.

This interest and research continued throughout his lifetime. He found that the violin and samisen shared a common ancestor —the ancient Egyptian *robanostron*.

There followed the foundation of a factory in Nagoya, specializing in the production of violins, with constant improvement in quality. When things went well, Masakichi could turn out 400 violins and 4,000 bows a day. The Suzuki violin factory employed 1,100 workers; the largest factory in Germany employed 200.[1]

Into this environment of thriving violin production was born Shinichi Suzuki—one of twelve children. Dr. Suzuki's days in elementary school and the commercial secondary school he attended are described in his book, *Nurtured by Love*. The picture that emerges is one of a sensitive, gifted, child, who lived, enjoyed, and groped for meaning in life. Important intellectual and spiritual influences were the sayings of the Buddhist priest Dogen and the writings of Tolstoy, particularly his *Diary*.

The young Suzuki was destined by the family to spend his days involved with the commercial enterprise of the factory. After graduating from Nagoya Commercial School, he took a position in the export section of the enterprise. It is the result of fate (or would Dr. Suzuki say "the work of the life force"?) and Dr. Suzuki's passionate search for self-knowledge and understanding that caused things to turn out differently.

Some foreshadowings of the intensity of soul Dr. Suzuki possessed can be glimpsed in *Nurtured by Love*. The image of the young Suzuki in 1904, listening to the stories told by the factory's night-shift workers as they polished violins, is not easily forgotten. Nor is the story of his effort to learn a Haydn Minuet on a violin procured from the factory, with a wind-up gramophone recording of Elman playing the Minuet as his only teacher. This, his first effort at violin playing, occurred before he graduated from commercial college. He practiced day after day until he finally was able to play the piece. He describes the result as "more a scraping than anything else."[2] How human is this urge to want to play an instrument, yet how rare the drive that motivates the attempt without teacher or music. Or is it so rare? Dr. Suzuki says such drive is at the core of every human being

After two years' work in packing and doing accounts while in charge of the export section of the factory, Dr. Suzuki fell ill and the physcian prescribed rest. Dr. Suzuki went to an inn at Ketnu to rest and recuperate for three months. There he became friends with a Mr. Yanigada, who had been at one time a schoolmate of the Marquis Tokugawa at the Gokushuin, a school for children of royal blood in Tokyo. Dr. Suzuki came to know Yanigada well during his three months' stay at the inn and became close to the man and his family.

The following summer Dr. Suzuki was invited to join an expedition, for biological research, to Chishima, led by the Marquis Tokugawa. Mr. Yanigada was a member of the expedition and had suggested that the young Suzuki accompany them. Dr. Suzuki's father approved and he joined the expedition, bringing his violin from which, at that time (and ever since, it would seem), he was inseparable. The expedition set sail on the first day of August 1919.

Miss Nobu Koda, a renowned pianist, was also on the expedition; her brother had been one of the first Japanese to set foot on the Northern Chishima Islands. There was a piano in the cabin of the *Chefu-Maru*, the expedition's 1,300-ton ship, and the 21-year-old Suzuki, tutored only by years of solitary work with the gramophone, played the violin accompanied by Miss Koda. Dr. Suzuki recalls this with some feelings of awkwardness.

The autumn following the cruise, Marquis Tokugawa appeared one day in Nagoya and suggested to Dr. Suzuki's father that Shinichi be allowed to study music. Miss Koda had said that he showed promise. Dr. Suzuki's father's response was, "He may like music, but...he will be obliged to kowtow to a lot of people in order to get on. If he wants to listen to music, he can become a successful businessman and hire those kind of people to come and play for him."[3] Dr. Suzuki was sure his father would not allow him to study violin.

This may seem much like the stereotyped financial opposition to music-as-a-career encountered by many famous Western composers and musicians, but there is a poignant difference. There is something very tender and human about the elder Suzuki's concern for his son. The vicious competition, back-biting, and cruel manipulation so unfortunately common in musical circles, seems almost to have been foreseen by Masakichi. It was this he feared for his son, not failure to produce financially. Another touching difference is the unique situation of Dr. Suzuki: ardently desiring to find the secret of the beautiful violin playing that so moved him when he listened to recordings, yet being so situated in time and space that such an undertaking might be considered nearly impossible.

But it was socially also nearly impossible for the elder Suzuki to say "no" to the Marquis Tokugawa. The name "Tokugawa" had been borne by shoguns for 200 years and was connected by marriage to the family of the Emperor himself. Thus, it is not without reason that Dr. Suzuki ascribes the unexpected change in his fate to the Marquis Tokugawa. In fact, he says, the Chishima expedition "decided my entire fate and led it in a new direction."[4]

Thus it was, that in the spring of 1920 at the age of twenty-one, Dr. Suzuki went to Tokyo to study violin with Ko Ando, the younger sister of Miss Koda. Dr. Suzuki was given a room in Marquis Tokugawa's mansion in Fujimi-Cho, Azabu and had his meals with the Marquis. Almost every day at the Tokugawa mansion there were visits from scholars and friends—the physicist Torahiku Terada, the phoneticist Kotaji Satsuda. Dr. Suzuki feels it was the Marquis' way of ensuring that his character was properly trained.[5]

14

At last Dr. Suzuki was being instructed in the art of violin playing. It had been a long struggle only to reach a beginning. With this struggle in mind, Dr. Suzuki's words at the end of *Nurtured By Love* reverberate with meaning. "I, too, am one of those people whose early life was damaged by the wrong kind of education. Most people could say the same. I have tried to remedy this, and from the time I was young, I have been working hard . . . to improve myself."[6]

But the real struggle was only beginning in the spring of 1920. Dr. Suzuki was at last studying violin but, to his bitter disappointment, he began to realize that the education available in Tokyo did not seem to result in the kind of violin playing that moved him so much when he listened to recordings. He planned to enroll in the Ueno Academy, as well as continuing with Miss Ando, and began studying diligently for the entrance examination. Shortly before he was to take the exam, he went to hear the music academy's graduation recital. He was bitterly disappointed. After hearing only the best performers of the world on records, the recital was a frightful letdown. Dr. Suzuki refused to go to the Academy. He said he preferred to continue studying privately with Miss Ando.

Here the sensitivity of Dr. Suzuki to his environment and his courage in following his perceptions can be seen as the individual's influence on fate. How many of us have submitted to mediocre training, burying and repressing our disappointment, rather than facing it and trying to do something to address the cause of those feelings. Perhaps not all of us have the financial freedom or cross-cultural opportunities to avail ourselves of what Dr. Suzuki did. Many of us are trapped by the educational systems of our times and society. We do not have the alternatives that Dr. Suzuki found, or at least can't see them. The real miracle of Dr. Suzuki is that he *made* his alternatives in a society much more structured in terms of individual fate, than our Western society is thought to be. And he found his alternatives through patient acceptance of what seemed his fate, yet with instant readiness to brave the unknown or refuse the mediocre when he had a real opportunity to do so.

So, Dr. Suzuki continued studying with Miss Ando and took lessons in music theory from Professor Ryntar Hirota and in acoustics from Professor H. Tanabe. Then, the Marquis began talking about taking a world tour. He expected to be gone about a year and invited Dr. Suzuki to come along. Dr. Suzuki was interested only in studying violin, however, and the matter was dropped.

At home for summer vacation, Dr. Suzuki mentioned the tour to his father. To Dr. Suzuki's surprise, his father thought the world tour an excellent idea and even said he could spare 150,000 yen for such an adventure. But Dr. Suzuki still preferred to continue his violin studies. The following autumn, in Tokyo, Dr. Suzuki recounted his father's offer to the Marquis over dinner. The Marquis flourished his chopsticks in midair and, with a twinkle in his eye, said, "Well done, Suzuki. You'd better grab that 150,000 yen. You can stop off in Germany and study violin."[7]

The Marquis went to Nagoya to work out details with the elder Suzuki. By October 1920, Dr. Suzuki was on board the luxury liner, *Hakone Maru*, enroute to Marseilles with the Marquis. The elder Suzuki had told the Marquis, "I am delighted to have you take my son with you, sir. By all means, let him study in Germany with whatever money is left over."[8]

Disappointed with the Ueno Music Academy in the spring, by autumn Dr. Suzuki was on his way to Germany to study. It was October 1920. Dr. Suzuki was twenty-two. The life force was shaping his destiny.

The post-World War I Germany to which Dr. Suzuki was enroute was in the throes of the tremendous inflation that led to the rise of Hitler and World War II. Dr. Suzuki's money went a long way, though it ultimately cost him more than 150,000 yen. He ended up spending eight years in Germany.

Dr. Suzuki said good-bye to the Marquis in Marseilles as soon as the *Hakone Maru* docked and went straight to Berlin. The Marquis went off on his world tour and Dr. Suzuki devoted himself to the pursuit of his chosen art.

He took a room at a hotel in Berlin and began the process of selecting a violin teacher. For three months he went to concerts every day. He had refused Professor Ando's offer of introductions. He preferred to listen until he heard a violinist play of whom he could truly say, "This is the person I want for a teacher." After three months he was on the verge of moving to Vienna. No performance had so moved him. Then he heard the Klingler Quartet. That was it. Klingler was the man with whom he would study.

This may all sound very matter-of-fact, yet it is truly remarkable. Oblivious to all the strata of auditions, credentials, and prerequisites, Dr. Suzuki selected his own master teacher (it is very much in the tradition of Zen) and then pursued him in spite of vast gaps in cultural tradition and bureaucratic approach. What is even more remarkable, he was successful.

Klingler, born in 1879, was not teaching private students that January of 1921 when Dr. Suzuki singled him out as his master teacher. Klingler had studied violin under Schuster and the great Joseph Joachim. He had studied composition with Max Bruch, been the concertmaster of the Berlin Symphony Orchestra, and violist in the Joachim Quartet. Now he was a master at the Berlin Music Academy and devoted to the artistic excellence of the Klingler Quartet. Yet, when Dr. Suzuki sent his note in English (he could not yet write German), "Please take me as your pupil," Klingler's response came the following Wednesday, "Come."[9] Says Suzuki:

> Klingler was forty, handsome, a man one could become extremely fond of. What he taught me was not so much technique as the real essence of music. For instance, if we were working on a Handel Sonata, he would

earnestly explain to me what great religious feeling Handel must have been filled with when he wrote it and then he would play it for me. He would look for the roots underlying a man and his art and lead me to them.[10]

Dr. Suzuki's lessons with Klingler usually lasted about two hours. During the first four years, he studied concertos and sonatas; the next four years, chamber music. At first, Dr. Suzuki was often in despair at the great amount of material he was assigned to cover. He felt he had no talent and found the many pieces assigned at each lesson an agony to try to perfect. He had not yet come to the realization that repetition was the essence of accomplishment; that it was just a matter of repeating a piece hundreds of times (given the help of a competent teacher) that would lead to competence, mastery, beauty, and perfection. Dr. Suzuki was often invited to concerts at Klingler's home and these, along with concerts at the home of his friend, Dr. Michaelis, he now considers as having had inestimable importance in his development.

It seems that, in a sense, Dr. Suzuki learned as much about art as about violin virtuosity during his years in Germany. The road that would lead to making virtuosity a possibility for anyone who cared to use Dr. Suzuki's approach was very much a result of Dr. Suzuki's unique insight and contribution. What he did find in the Germany of the '20s was regard for the individual person, and the respect for the humanity that is inherent in great art.

Dr. Michaelis, a professor of medicine, had visited the Suzukis in Nagoya when he was in Japan and returned their hospitality by befriending the young Suzuki in Berlin. He was an accomplished pianist and often accompanied his wife, who had studied singing at the Vienna Music Academy. Once, at a home concert, Dr. Suzuki heard his wife whisper to him, "Please play a half a tone lower," because she had a bit of a cold. "Yes, dear,"[11] Michaelis replied, and without a moment's hesitation transposed a difficult song by Brahms, playing a semitone lower without the music. Dr. Suzuki was astonished at this ability.

Michaelis accepted an invitation to become a dean at Johns Hopkins University in the United States, but felt concerned about leaving the young man. He asked a friend to keep an eye on him; the friend was Dr. Albert Einstein.

At a farewell dinner party given by Michaelis, Dr. Suzuki had been asked to play. He felt a bit sheepish but played the Bruch Concerto. Afterwards, an elderly German lady commented, "Suzuki grew up in Japan in a completely different environment to ours. But in spite of that, his performance clearly expressed to me the Germanness of Bruch. Tell me, is such a thing possible?" There was an embarrassed silence. Finally, Dr. Einstein said quietly, "People are all the same, Madame."[12] Dr. Suzuki was tremendously moved.

Einstein then befriended Dr. Suzuki. Often, when there was a good concert in town, Einstein would telephone and say, "I have tickets, so let's go."[13] This happened before a Bach concert and Einstein and Dr. Suzuki arranged to meet at a certain time at the bus stop. Dr. Suzuki arrived right on time but the eminent scholar was there before him. "Even though I was a mere stripling, he had invited me as his guest and treated me accordingly. I just bowed and did not know what to do."[14]

The humaneness and decency of such eminent people made a profound impression on Dr. Suzuki. Einstein he admired, not only as a scientist and human being, but also as a musician:

> Einstein was an acknowledged virtuoso on the violin. He never went anywhere without his violin. His specialities such as the Bach Chaconne, were magnificent—his light, flowing finger movement, his beautifully delicate tone. In comparison with his playing,

mine, though I tried to keep in mind that I must play effortlessly and with ease, seemed to me a constant struggle.[15]

It was not only Einstein, all the members of this circle were prominent people in their fields, yet they all loved art and were extremely modest and kind:

Here was I, just a beginner of no particular talent, a mere struggling student, and never once did they make me feel foolish or treat me lightly . . . they accepted me warmly and made sure I enjoyed myself . . . they took pains to include me in the conversation and to see I was not bored.[16]

The influence of these people was indeed great. "Although they did not tell it to me in so many words, Michaelis, the physician, and Einstein, the scientist, graphically brought home to me what the study of music can do for a person. . . ."[17]

I want Japanese children to grow up to be people who have this pleasure in their lives . . . to be people of as high intellect and sensitivity . . . the purpose of talent education is to train children, not to be professional musicians but to be fine musicians and to show high ability in any other field they enter.[18]

Dr. Suzuki clearly feels the excellence and achievement of such men as Michaelis and Einstein is related to the excellence they achieved in music. The phrase, "This matchless beauty of Einstein's mathematics," suggests to him a beauty of conception that was the outcome of pure musical skill. Einstein was sixteen when the idea that was to bring about a revolution in the science of physics occurred to him. Einstein himself said,

"It occurred to me by intuition, and music is the driving force behind this intuition. My parents had me study the violin from the time I was six. My new discovery is the result of musical perception." [19]

It is greatness of soul that Dr. Suzuki seeks to impart through talent education. Such greatness comes from within the individual and is a potential that every human being possesses. The teacher counsels and facilitates the self-realization of that potential. Spiritual forces come into play as the student is guided with love and respect. Mastery of an instrument is Dr. Suzuki's specialty. What the student will do with the greatness of soul developed to achieve mastery remains entirely up to the individual.

How misguided are they who seize upon Dr. Suzuki's innovations to develop petulant virtuosi buried in selfish showing off. Instead of greatness of soul, greatness of ego develops. Greatness of ego, I might add, not only of the violinist but also of the violinists' parents and teachers. As Dr. Suzuki might say with characteristic understatement, "This is a mistake: a great mistake."

Yet perhaps it is as with the unique contribution of other great innovators—Jesus Christ, Karl Marx. The systems and bureaucracies that are built (ostensibly) on their ideas would be a great disappointment to their originators if they could see them today. Let us hope that such will not be the case with Dr. Suzuki.

In addition to his work with Klingler, Dr. Suzuki also studied intensively by listening to recordings of the great violin works played by various masters. In particular, he spent long hours listening to the playing of Fritz Kreisler while refining a bow technique that is uniquely Dr. Suzuki's. The main focus of his listening was the beautiful sound. He experimented extensively with how to produce this beautiful sound and has evolved a bow technique that emphasizes whole-arm movement rather than segmentalized movement: a slightly dropped elbow

21

for depth of tone and string changes based on action of the elbow and wrist. This produces a sound that validates the Suzuki saying, "Tone has living soul."

The importance Dr. Suzuki accords to listening is inherent in the many hours he himself spent in intensely concentrated listening as he developed his bow technique. These hours are also the genesis of that familiar expression, "Place the bow on the Kreisler Highway, please." This is the particular area between the bridge and fingerboard that produces the best tone quality for most playing and the right conditions for "living soul" to express. Suzuki students are continuously reminded to "stay on the Kreisler Highway."

Dr. Suzuki's ability to help his students develop a beautiful tone and the bowing technique he has developed are among the main reasons that Suzuki teachers come to Matsumoto to study with him. Many of the Suzuki pedagogical techniques can be learned by reading or hearing about them from others. It is very difficult to develop the tone quality or the bowing technique unless you study directly with Dr. Suzuki or someone who has studied with Dr. Suzuki (and mastered the technique).

Dr. Suzuki says he was studying Kreisler records intensively in Tokyo (upon his return from Berlin) before he taught his first young students, and he continued the intensive study for about ten years. He continues to study tone in this way up to the present time, using the cello sounds of Pablo Casals as another model to emulate.

Another important insight came to Dr. Suzuki in Berlin. He was amazed at the mastery little children showed of their native tongue. He recounts how difficult and discouraging was his effort to gain command of the German language. It was particularly distressing, he recalls, to see little two- and three-year-olds running about, babbling with the greatest ease and fluency in German while he had to struggle with each syllable and grammatical pattern. His distress changed to respect and admiration and wondering why we could not instruct children in other difficult things as thoroughly and easily as parents seemed to be able to teach them their native tongue. This was one of the generating experiences that led ultimately to the development of the "mother tongue method."

Another important event took place in Berlin. Dr. Suzuki met his wife. She studied voice in Berlin and belonged to a musical family. Both her brother and her sister played musical instruments. They met Dr. Suzuki in music circles in Berlin (Dr. Suzuki was the first Japanese person Mrs. Suzuki had ever met) and began playing chamber music together. In fact, it was at one of the home concerts mentioned earlier that they met. Mrs. Suzuki recalls the consternation the proposed marriage caused in both families. Dr. Suzuki's elder brother was dispatched from Nagoya (ostensibly on business) to decide whether the family should give permission for Dr. Suzuki's marriage to a foreign girl. Dr. Suzuki was much beloved by the girl's immediate family, her mother, brother and sister, but there were objections and concern from other members of the family, particularly as Japan was such a little-known country in Europe at that time. Even her mother was concerned about her going so very far away; there were no air routes in those days. It was a very big step. They thought Dr. Suzuki was so wonderful that consent was finally given, but not without some relatives threatening to boycott the wedding. In the end, however, they all came, to a beautiful church ceremony that took place in Berlin on February 8, 1928.

Dr. Suzuki's mother was taken ill in 1929 and he and his bride returned to Japan via Siberian train and ship. That same year, the bank crash in New York caused severe financial losses to the family. When the Suzukis first arrived, the disaster had not yet hit and they enjoyed a happy family reunion. (Perhaps it is not quite correct to say the disaster had not hit. Dr. Suzuki's father wished to shield the family from the blow and tried to carry on by borrowing money from Japanese money lenders.)

Mrs. Suzuki recalls the family had a big black Packard, driven by a chauffeur. She and Dr. Suzuki had their own home and five maids to care for it.

Nagoya was quite a challenge for Mrs. Suzuki. She was the only foreigner in the city and spoke no Japanese. She was young and pretty, and people would stare at her whenever she went out. The Suzuki family was prominent in the Nagoya area, which didn't help her to feel any less conspicuous.

One can only be filled with admiration for both Suzukis at the courageous step their marriage represented. Marriage to foreigners was an unheard of thing in both Japan and Germany. Japan was, in fact, almost unknown to the Western world. It had been only in 1853—just forty-five years before Dr. Suzuki's birth—that Admiral Perry sailed into the Sea of Japan and insisted some sort of relationship be set up between Japan and the Western world.

It is also a testimony to both families that they gave their permission for what was to become a marriage of destiny. It was the custom in Japan at that time for families to arrange the marriages of their children. There seems to have been some change here in Masakichi, who some years earlier had to be gently hoodwinked with the help of royal personages into allowing his son to study violin rather than devote his life to business. The matter of allowing a son to marry a foreigner of his own choosing seems almost revolutionary, but perhaps he recognized just what sort of person this son really was.

When the worldwide financial disaster of 1929 hit the family, the young Suzukis decided it was necessary to earn a living. There were more possibilities in Tokyo than in Matsumoto, and they moved there in 1930. Their circumstances were difficult, because there was little money and Mrs. Suzuki was still struggling with the language. There was no money to hire a tutor so she began learning Japanese on her own. There were more foreigners in Tokyo than in Matsumoto, so occasionally Mrs. Suzuki could speak German or English. There was more interest in Western classical music in Tokyo, as well.

Dr. Suzuki taught at the Imperial Music School in Tokyo, and also at the Kunitachi Music School. His students were the usual teenagers and adults. One of his adult students, however, asked Dr. Suzuki to teach his four-year-old, Tochiya Eto. It was for Eto that Dr. Suzuki requested of his brother at the Nagoya Violin Factory that a violin small enough to comfortably fit a four-year-old be constructed. It was for Eto that Dr. Suzuki began choosing and selecting pieces that such a little one could learn from and enjoy. Eto, by the way, went on to become a concert violinist and eventually a professor at Curtis Institute in the United States.

Koji Toyoda also studied with Dr. Suzuki in Tokyo. Upon Dr. Suzuki's return from Berlin, he had undertaken the task of teaching violin in Nagoya. Koji's father lived in Hammamatsu, but when Dr. Suzuki moved to Tokyo, Mr. Toyoda also moved there with his entire family.

Little Koji studied attentively at the Suzuki home in Tokyo. Dr. Suzuki says of his tiny student:

> It was a result of circumstances that he played the violin. Whether he liked it or disliked it is not the question. Precisely as all Japanese children learn the Japanese language, and learn it by heart, to like or dislike had no bearing at all. It was exactly the same. Koji was brought up, listening every day to records. It was no strain for him to practice really well. Good practicing is sure to produce fine results; that is why three-year-old Koji played "Humoresque" so well, and not because he was a genius.[20]

Koji went on to become the first Japanese concert master of the Berlin Symphony Orchestra. He first played on stage in 1935, when Dr. Suzuki's students gave a performance at the Nihon Seinenkan in Tokyo. Toshiya Eto was then seven. Eto played the Seitz Violin Concerto No. 3 that night, accompanied by the Tokyo string orchestra. Koji, with his 1/16 violin in hand, played "Humoresque." Koji was hailed the next day as a genius, somewhat to Dr. Suzuki's chagrin. He had told the journalists:

> Talent is not inherited or inborn, but trained and educated. Genius is an honorific name given to those who are brought up and trained to high ability.[21]

Perhaps "genius" is also a word that sells newspapers. In any case, Dr. Suzuki has had to struggle continually with the concept that he has somehow happened on a happy collection of geniuses rather than that he has found a way of nurturing a very high level of achievement in every person.

In 1939, Dr. Suzuki's young students were progressing remarkably. Toshiya at eleven received the first prize in a Ministry of Education music contest sponsored through the Mainichi newspapers. The contest piece was Bach's A-Minor Concerto, now one of the Suzuki graduation pieces, the core of the seventh volume in the curriculum.

The curriculum began to be formed while Dr. Suzuki worked with his young students in Tokyo before the war and recognized what suited their development and what did not. The "Humoresque" played by Koji at three, that so captivated the Japanese press in 1935, is now a part of Volume III. The Seitz played by Eto (age seven) that same night has not been included in the curriculum. Movements from the Seitz Student Concertos Nos. 2 and 5 are included in Volume IV, but the Seitz No. 3 didn't make it.

The night Toshiya won first prize for the Bach A-Minor, Dr. Suzuki asked that the judges listen to someone else but not score him. This someone was Koji, who at seven could also play the Bach A-Minor and performed it beautifully. This, Dr. Suzuki insisted, was the result of education—not genius.

For as long as Dr. Suzuki remained in Tokyo after World War II had spread there, most of his young students refused to be evacuated. The air raids worsened. Mrs. Suzuki urged her husband to move to Hakone, where they had a small cottage near Lake Ashi they had used for fishing. Finally, he agreed.

As it turned out, Mrs. Suzuki was sent to Hakone, and Dr. Suzuki went to distant Kiso-Fukushima to work in a wood factory. Although Mrs. Suzuki was a Japanese subject by marriage, all foreigners were looked upon with extreme suspicion. The Germans in Japan were evacuated to the mountain resorts of Karnizawa and Hakone much as the Japanese in the United States were placed in "settlements" in California. It did not matter that Germany was an ally. Mrs. Suzuki could not accompany her husband to Kiso-Fukushima, though he could visit her from time to time.

It was 1943 and Dr. Suzuki was forty-five. The German army was defeated at Stalingrad and the Japanese army was forced to withdraw from Guadalcanal. Dr. Suzuki's father had converted the violin factory to make seaplane floats, but the supply of Japanese cypress wood needed for the floats was no longer available. It was decided that Dr. Suzuki would supervise the obtaining of lumber from the Kiso-Fukushima forests near the Nagoya factory.

And so it was that he went to live alone among the mountains of Kiso-Fukushima and convert a *geta* (Japanese wooden sandal) factory into a lumber yard to supply the float factory in Nagoya. He was able to get first-class timber from the forest, which they sawed and sent off to Nagoya. Dr. Suzuki mentions that in his youth a Zen priest named Dogen had taught him to live as best he could, no matter what happened—to throw himself into a work at hand and gain from it. This he did at the lumber mill.

The work was carried out cheerfully but living conditions grew worse and worse. Finally, the distribution of provisions came to a standstill. At this hard time, his younger sister, who had lost her husband, came with her two young children to live with Dr. Suzuki. On factory holidays, they would go into the mountains to look for bracken water or water algae. This, boiled into a kind of gruel, helped them appease hunger.

At the factory, meals and living conditions were miserable. Everyone worked desperately hard each day, with little to look forward to. Dr. Suzuki played the violin for the factory workers each morning in the clear mountain air. He felt responsible for them and could think of nothing else to do that might help.

The years of the war were indeed a terrible time for the Suzukis. There was no time for music as Japan became embroiled in the all-out war effort. The Nagoya Violin Factory was bombed and one of the beloved Suzuki brothers was killed during the raid. He was a kind of civil defense warden and was killed while performing this duty during the bombing.

At last the war ended. But not trouble. Dr. Suzuki heard that both of Koji's parents had died. Koji's family had moved to Tokyo because of Dr. Suzuki and he felt responsible for Koji. Hurriedly, he sent a letter of inquiry to their old address in Tokyo. There was no answer. He asked the radio station to broadcast on their missing-persons program: "Koji Toyoda, I am in Kiso-Fukushima. Please let me know where you are."

Two months later a letter arrived from a man named Toyoda. It was Koji's uncle; he had taken care of Koji. Dr. Suzuki wrote at once and soon afterward Koji, now eleven, came with his uncle to Kiso-Fukushima.

The uncle ran a small sake drinking place in Hamamatsu. Koji had not played violin for three years while he helped his uncle in the shop. The uncle begged Dr. Suzuki to take care of Koji, then left him. From that day, Koji became a member of the Suzuki family.

Family members were glad to have Koji live with them at Kiso-Fukushima. The group now consisted of seven people: Dr. Suzuki, his aunt with her girl helper, his sister, and the three children.

Dr. Suzuki dates the beginning of Talent Education in 1945 with the end of World War II. That year marked the end of his three-year stay in Kiso-Fukushima. In Matsumoto at this time there was talk among the culture-minded of founding a music school. Mrs. Tamiki Mori, a singer who had taught with Dr. Suzuki at the Imperial Music School in Tokyo, had evacuated to Matsumoto and was among the planners. She sent a message to Dr. Suzuki in Kiso-Fukushima suggesting that he come to Matsumoto and help with the founding of the proposed school. This was his reply.

> I am not very interested in doing repair work on people who can play already. I did enough of that before in Tokyo. What I want to try is infant education. I have worked out a new method I want to teach to small children—not to turn out geniuses but through violin playing, to extend the child's ability. I have been doing this research for many years. That is why I want to put all my efforts into this kind of education in the future. If my idea finds approval, I will help with teaching along these lines.[22]

Word came back that those interested in starting a school had consented to Dr. Suzuki's terms. Thus it was that he left Kiso-Fukushima for Matsumoto. At first he commuted between the two cities; then finally he moved, and the Talent Education Movement thus began at the Matsumoto Music School. But Dr. Suzuki had another battle on his hands before he could devote himself wholly to music. He had had a stomach ailment since his twenties and his physical condition was very unsatisfactory by the end of the war.

To recuperate, he rented a room in Asoma Spa, a suburb of Matsumoto, and went to live there by himself. Mrs. Suzuki made her way to Matsumoto to see him. She had been given a job with the American Red Cross in Yokohama, where the occupation forces had set up their headquarters. Separation was unpleasant indeed, but Mrs. Suzuki's income was vital to the family. Money was frozen at that point and the amount that people were allowed to withdraw was infinitesimal. It was decided she must keep her job for the good of all.

Dr. Suzuki's condition continued to deteriorate and finally he sent for his sister in Kiso-Fukushima. When Mrs. Suzuki next visited she was shocked at his condition and wanted to stay and care for him. Dr. Suzuki's sister promised to stay and look after him and begged Mrs. Suzuki to go on working for the Red Cross, or they would all starve. Reluctantly, she agreed but visited whenever possible, despite a trip that meant nine hours of standing in a crowded, smoky train.

The doctor's diagnosis was atony (enervation, langour) of the stomach. Dr. Suzuki suffered violent pain and loss of both physical and mental perception. Finally, he became totally bedridden.

One day a piano teacher from the Matsumoto Music School, Miss Misako Koike, came to visit him. She was horrified at his condition and immediately summoned a doctor of Chinese medicine.

The Chinese doctor, Mrs. Uehara, contrary to the previous doctor's instructions which prescribed only rice gruel or Western-style soup, told Dr. Suzuki to eat unpolished rice and pickled vegetables. Confronted with death, he followed Mrs. Uehara's regime. The diet reactivated his stomach. In one week he was able to stand up and within a month could walk (slowly) outside.

While convalescing, Dr. Suzuki invented a new system for calculating basic arithmetic operations: multiplication, division, addition, subtraction. Eventually the system was tested by the Ministry of Education (in 1954) and included in the curriculum of many elementary schools in Japan. At the time, Dr. Suzuki thought it would be something he could use in his talent education plan when he recovered.

Dr. Suzuki did recover and was at last able to devote himself wholly to trying to put into use the method he had developed. The entire Kiso-Fukushima family moved to Matsumoto to be with. Hina Suzuki was like a mother to young Koji who continued to be a part of their family.

The first year, there were three six-year-olds in the farming community of Matsumoto who studied with Dr. Suzuki. The ravages of the war were still being felt and there was only one violin to be shared between the three. As one completed his daily practice, he would run with the violin to the house of the next in line. Since Dr. Suzuki believed then, as now, "the day you don't practice is the day you don't eat," this must have been a very good way to ensure that daily practice did take place.

Dr. Suzuki was back, teaching full steam now, but was not too happy with the acoustics in Japanese style housing. Anyone knowing his love for pure sound (one of his 1977 Kanji mottoes was "Tone has Living Soul") can appreciate how important acoustics would be to him. The ubiquitous Japanese tatami mats did not reflect sound waves with a beauty that satisfied him; in fact, they tended to absorb rather than reflect and send back sound.

Accordingly, the Suzukis decided to build a Western-style house with a large music room that would have the very best acoustics they could devise. Mrs. Suzuki continued working until this house was built and furnished. Dr. Suzuki began teaching at home and a talent education preschool experiment was located in his home as well. It was not until

1967 that the present Talent Education Institute was built. John Kendall, one of the first Americans to study Dr. Suzuki's teaching method, came to Matsumoto in 1959 and studied with Dr. Suzuki before the Institute was built. Mrs. Suzuki handled all the correspondence at that time. In 1978, there was an office staff of ten at the Institute to handle business affairs. Ten years later, the office staff numbered fifteen.

Dr. Suzuki continues to guide the Talent Education Movement with the goal of altering the course of world education for the better. Based on the way one learns one's native tongue, it is a system in which no one is left behind. It is a system based on love. It fosters truth, joy, and beauty in each child's character. It teaches children to be warm and loving to others, to cooperate rather than compete.

This is a magnificent goal and a goal whose urgency is attested to by many modern movements. Dr. James Gordon, in his *Parent Effectiveness Training* and *Teacher Effectiveness Training* books, attests to the destructive effect of much, or even most, compulsory education. Writers Neil Postman and C. Weingartner, in *Teaching as a Subversive Activity,* and John Holt in *How Children Fail,* document the horrifying effects that present systems of education can have on people. Dr. John Bradshaw, in his book *Bradshaw: On the Family* and in several PBS television series, sees the family as the agency that created Dachow and Auschwitz. In an interview in *New Age Journal,* Bradshaw comments, "We have been absolutely on the wrong course. We've been systematically repressing emotions for hundreds of years." Dr. Suzuki, too, perceives this problem and has made his own unique contribution to alleviating it.

Strength to carry out his vision came in part from the rubble and destruction of World War II for Dr. Suzuki. After the War, when the remains of many destroyed buildings were seen all over Japan, he started his movement, realizing how innocent children were suffering from the dreadful mistakes made by adults. These precious children had no part in the war, yet they were suffering the most; not only in lack of proper food, clothing and homes, but more importantly, in education. The motto Dr. Suzuki adopted for the Talent Education Movement was "For the Happiness of All Children."

This is one of the basic tenets of the Talent Education Movement, which Dr. Suzuki intends as an alternative to educational systems that result in world wars and weapons of mass destruction. The use of music as a civilizing agent for the human soul, the use of the discipline of learning an instrument to mastery as a way to teach right action, ultimately results in the happiness, the spiritual joy that Dr. Suzuki made the motto of talent education.

Dr. Suzuki continued his work with his young students. Koji Toyoda went on to concertize, play string quartets with Grumiaux, and become concertmaster of the Berlin Radio Symphony Orchestra. Toshiyo Ito won Japan's prestigious Mainichi Shinbun award at the age of eleven, and is now known throughout the world as an outstanding soloist. The three Kabayashi brothers each became concertmaster of a major symphony: Takeshi, Concertmaster of the Czechoslovakian Symphony; Kenji, Concertmaster of the Oklahoma Symphony; Urakawa, Concertmaster of the Bamberg Symphony. Many of Dr. Suzuki's students from those early days became symphony musicians, playing with the NHK Symphony, the Stuttgart Symphony, the Munich Symphony.

Training professional musicians has not been Dr. Suzuki's aim, however. "I have never pressed my young charges to enter the professional field. That is not my aim in education."[22] Dr. Suzuki's much broader aim has been to pursue and develop the method through which all children can be fully developed in their abilities.

In his 1977 bulletin, prepared for the Second International Conference on Talent Education, held in Hawaii, Dr. Suzuki makes the following declaration.

Because of the fact that children all over the world prove their ability in learning their own mother tongue, we firmly believe that ability is not inherited, but is possible to be equally acquired by every child. However, to our great sorrow, because of wrong teaching methods, human beings have failed in their attempt to fully develop children's high potentialities with the only exception being the mother tongue acquirement method. What's worse, people have failed to realize their own faults in that they have used the wrong methods of teaching children and attributed their failure to the lack of inherent ability in the children. That is the history of ignorance and thoughtlessness of human beings in the past. They have made serious mistakes, but now is the time when we should go ahead and shift to a new era of awakening for humanity, holding this firm belief, and love for humanity, as the pioneers of a new era in which every child can be developed properly.[24]

CHAPTER 2

GROWTH OF THE TALENT EDUCATION
MOVEMENT

That Dr. Suzuki had started a new educational movement with violin teaching became known to various parents in the Nagoya area. A grandmother appeared one day at the Matsumoto Music School with her granddaughter, Hiroko, aged six. Hiroko had lived in a remote part of Manchuria as a tiny child and had been repatriated after the war. She was very slow in all she did. The grandmother wanted to know if Dr. Suzuki could help the girl.

Dr. Suzuki undertook the task but found it no small challenge. Hiroko-Chan was indeed slow. Whatever she did could stand no comparison with what other children of the same age did.

On the second floor of the school, Dr. Suzuki aligned Hiroko with other children of her age group and played a favorite game. "Attention everybody. When I call one, two, three, put your right hand on top of your head as fast as you can; at the word 'three' remember, not before or after."[25] Hiroko was the only child who was slow in getting her hand to her head. She took her time as if time were nonexistent. More than wanting to teach the child to play the violin, Dr. Suzuki wanted to help her speed up her reactions.

The game was played many more times in the next years. Hiroko-Chan learned to move more quickly, to play the violin. Eventually, Hiroko Yamado became the only Japanese woman to play in the Berlin Radio Orchestra.

During the years in Tokyo before the war, Dr. Suzuki had taught a blind child to play. His parents brought him to Dr. Suzuki at the age of five. When pondering whether to attempt this or not, Dr. Suzuki realized he often played with his eyes closed. "Yes, I will make little Teichi see the violin, strings, and bow. He doesn't need physical eyes if I can teach him to use his spiritual ones." [26]

That Dr. Suzuki chose to stay in Matsumoto and devote himself to teaching small children rather than return to Tokyo after World War II to pick up the threads of a professional artist's career is a remarkable fact from a worldly point of view. His motivation seems to have been to share with little ones what he had learned after nearly fifty years of struggling. He wanted to help small children have a chance at the mastery, achievement, and human kindness he had observed and so admired in music circles in Berlin.

In a sense, what Dr. Suzuki saw in Berlin was the very epitome of Western achievement. Einstein and Michaelis were great scientists, great innovators in the fields of physics and medicine; they were also fine musicians. What was the link? Dr. Suzuki wanted to find this link between innovation, artistry, humanitarianism. He wanted to help others along paths toward such development but his own experience gave him the conviction that these paths were not easily found in the halls of bureaucratized academe. Nor was the answer to be found in devoting himself to a concertizing career or to use his teaching ideas to turn out a few very fine violinists whom the world could hail as geniuses and who would describe their teacher as a master teacher of geniuses. That was not what Dr. Suzuki saw as a meaningful life's achievement. He wanted to prove his conviction that everyone had the potential to tread such paths of achievement.

The years passed and Dr. Suzuki taught and worked with his little students. Other violin teachers observed his success and joined him, using his methods and curriculum. All interested students were accepted without auditions. Dr. Suzuki involved the parents of the little ones, having the mother learn to play first in order to motivate a tiny one to want to play the violin. He asked that his little students be immersed in the sound of the pieces they were learning. They heard records or tapes and then tried to play what they had heard.

In 1953, eight years after the date Dr. Suzuki has affixed (1945) as the beginning of the Talent Education Movement, Georges Duhamel, a French poet, dramatist, and novelist, was in Japan and heard a violin performance by the children of the Nagoya Branch, led by Professor Nishizaki. Duhamel wrote an article entitled "Ideal Childhood," describing the experience. He heard thirty children between the ages of six and ten play a Vivaldi concerto; he felt it to be a superb performance and was moved and entranced. He was impressed with a Bach piece the children played, as well, and was completely taken with a performance of a Mozart piece by one of the tiny students.

There were some rather odd remarks in the article such as "In spite of their handicap[?] of being Oriental and Japanese, these children have been trained to heights only attained by the most superior children in Europe." [27] But at least Duhamel was honest enough to record his amazement and admiration. These children out-performed "superior" European children; yet they had not been auditioned, given I.Q. tests, or specially screened in any way. Dr. Suzuki's contention that every child has tremendous potential had been demonstrated. Also he had shown that, with proper education and training, that potential could be realized.

In 1955, Dr. Suzuki's Talent Education pupils gave their first concert in Tokyo. This has become an annual event, with thousands of young violinists participating. Dr. Suzuki mentions the first concert rather matter-of-factly in *Nurtured by Love*, but apparently it was a rather electrifying event, or so it was described by Rognor Snedshund, Consul General of Finland in Japan. After hearing the 1955 Concert, he wrote the following account of the program:

The scene is Tokyo's new Sportshall on a Sunday in March. The galleries are full of 10,000 spectators who, spellbound, are following the spectacle in the arena where 1,200 violin playing children of the age of 4 to 15 are playing Vivaldi's Concerto in A minor. In the middle of the arena there is a platform with a grand piano and on the four sides thereof the youngest children are lined up.

The program was commenced by the first movement of Mozart's Violin Concerto in A major played by the eighty most advanced violinists. Thereupon, 120 of the next lower class joined them for playing the first movement of Bach's Concerto in A minor. And for each new item on the program a new group marched in until the total reached 1,200. After the Vivaldi Concerto the program consisted of various selections of Bach, Lully and Handel.

Behind this concert there is an all-Japan organization for 'the education of the children's talents." It has its headquarters in Matsumoto, Nagano Prefecture, and 65 branches in various parts of Japan. The total number of pupils is at present about 4,000. The founder and leader of this organization is a well-known violin teacher, Shinichi Suzuki, who naturally conducted this concert.

Everyone who was present at the concert in Tokyo Sportshall must have found it an eloquent testimony of the possibilities of bringing to light and developing children's talents at a tender age. And everyone of the audience is no doubt willing to subscribe to the statement by William James quoted in the program as follows:

"Compared with what we ought to be we are only half awake. We are making use of only a small part of our physical and mental resources. Stating the thing broadly the human individual thus lives far within his limits. He possesses powers of various sorts which he habitually fails to use." [28]

Also in 1955, Zen-On Music published Dr. Suzuki's ten-volume curriculum. This series is published by Zen-On in Japan to the present day. Summy-Birchard Inc. is the publisher for the world except Japan. The first eight volumes included companion recordings so that students could hear the pieces on which they were working beautifully played, concurrently with learning them. The pieces are now also available on companion audio cassettes and compact discs; students hear and know the pieces intimately as listeners *before* learning to play them. The emphasis is on playing, not reading or sight-reading.

A film was made at the 1955 concert. Apparently, it was as electrifying to music teachers as the original concert had been for its audience in Tokyo. It was a seven-minute film of the children playing Bach's *Double Violin Concerto*. This film was taken by Kenji Mochizuki, a student in the Oberlin Graduate School of Theology, to Professor Clifford A. Cook of the Oberlin College Conservatory.

Cook was so impressed that he arranged for Mochizuki to show the film and speak in classes at Oberlin College, and to appear before the Ohio String Teachers Association meeting in Oberlin in 1958. This was the spark that started the movement in the United States, where it has become more and more widely accepted and acclaimed, perhaps even more so than in Japan. [29]

One Ohio string teacher, John Kendall of Muskinguin College, Ohio, became so interested after seeing the film that he went to Japan in the summer of 1959 to investigate the teaching that produced such remarkable results. Kendall stayed in Matsumoto for a month. He returned to the United States, greatly impressed, and gave lectures in many areas of the country advocating the Suzuki Method. In 1961 he began publishing his *Listen and Play* series, using Dr. Suzuki's curriculum and based on Dr. Suzuki's philosophy.

In 1961, an event of great importance to Dr. Suzuki occurred. The great cellist Pablo Casals listened to 400 of Dr. Suzuki's pupils, aged five to twelve, playing for Casals at Tokyo's Bunkyo Hall. When the performance was over, Casals threw his arms around Dr. Suzuki and wept. The important thing was that Casals had responded to the beauty of education and the beauty of the children's outpouring of their vitality through music. Casals understood what was happening. Said Dr. Suzuki, "How often I myself had wept at this beautiful, innocent outpouring of the children's inner life force! Now the great seventy-five-year-old maestro himself was speechless in this sublime moment before the sound of that life force." [30]

In 1964, Dr. Suzuki and a party of nineteen invited by the American String Teachers Association, toured the United States giving concerts and lectures. Of this group, ten were students ages five to fourteen. They spent two weeks visiting universities in sixteen cities, giving twenty-six concerts and lectures.

Newsweek, March 25th, 1964, carried the following report.

"Fiddling Legions"

Seven-year-old Asako Hata playfully dropped a chunk of ice down her neighbor's back, and the long table of children at lunch one day last week burst into delighted giggles. Forty minutes later, Asako was standing on the stage of New York's august Juilliard School of Music, bobbing her head shyly to acknowledge the thunderous clapping that greeted her performance of a complicated Veracini sonata. The solo climaxed a concert that was at once impressive and absurd, in which ten tiny Japanese children, ranging in age from 5 to 14 played Bach and Vivaldi that drew bravos from a highly critical audience of Juilliard students and faculty. If their applause was tinged with sentimentality (when the children's teacher, Professor Shinichi Suzuki, stepped on stage to tune a 5-year-old's quarter-size violin, the audience sighed), it was nonetheless wholly deserved. "This is amazing," said Juilliard violin Professor Ivan Galamian. "They show remarkable training, a wonderful feeling for the rhythm and flow of music."

Playing without a conductor and using no scores, the youngsters were a living testimonial to the validity of Suzuki's unorthodox teaching method. He starts his children about 3, but the first lessons are for the child's mother. She comes once a week with her youngster, and after three months has normally progressed to "Twinkle, Twinkle, Little Star." "By that time," Suzuki explains in a mixture of German and English as expressive as his face, "the child has watched the mother play and wants to imitate her." Only then is the pupil given a pint-size violin. Through exposure to classical recordings and constant repetition, the child is ready to tackle simple Bach gavottes within a year. The 150,000 children Suzuki's system has trained in 30 years are far from robots. They combine virtuosity with feeling so successfully that when Pablo Casals heard a Suzuki recital in Tokyo, he rushed to the stage, shouting 'bravo,' and hugged the children.

Although about 5 per cent of Suzuki's students make careers in music, the 65-year-old professor insists: "I just want to make good citizens. If a child hears good music from the day of his birth, and learns to play it himself, he develops sensitivity, discipline and endurance. He gets a beautiful heart." Suzuki thoughtfully crinkled a few of the paper-wrapped candies he carries for his musicians. "If nations cooperate in raising good children, perhaps there won't be any war."

Suzuki has done more than revolutionize violin teaching in Japan. Oberlin Professor Clifford Cook says: "What Suzuki has done for young children earns him a place among the benefactors of mankind, along with Schweitzer, Casals, and Tom Dooley." [31]

By 1965, the annual All-Japan Concert had been shown on European television. Koji Toyoda wrote from Berlin that people who saw the performance by 1,800 children on television were astonished and could not believe it to be true. Koji, by the way, had been appointed Concertmaster of the Berlin Symphony Orchestra in 1962.

The success story has continued to the present day. There are so many Suzuki Institutes in the U.S. each summer that a diligent Suzuki family could spend the entire summer going from one to the next, and some do. Teacher training institutes are conducted at major universities each summer: Catholic University and George Mason University in the

Washington, D.C. area are examples. Student concerts and festivals abound. The concert at the famous Wolf Trap Filene Center for the Performing Arts was "limited" to 500 violinists from the Washington D.C. area for the 1987 concert because everyone interested in performing simply could not be accommodated. The 1988 performance at the Kennedy Center had to be similarly circumscribed, as did the 1993 Festival in Constitution Hall.

CHAPTER 3

DR. SUZUKI'S EDUCATIONAL PHILOSOPHY

In a talk given to the Japan Institute of Educational Psychology in 1973, Dr. Suzuki recounts how he began developing educational theory:

> It was forty years ago when this astonishing fact occurred to me. Children everywhere in the world were speaking in their own language; moreover, they did this fluently which required a very high level of proficiency . . . why did it appear that the mother tongue ability could be taught with the greatest of ease to every child . . . and yet why did they not do well in various subjects at school, acquiring this learning just as they did their language?[32]

Dr. Suzuki concluded that the discrepancy between what would seem an indicator of great mental ability—a child's ability to speak its native tongue proficiently and fluently—and what would seem to be an indicator of lack of ability—failure to do well in school subjects—was due to a difference in educational methods. He further speculated that if children were taught any subject in the same way they had been taught to speak their native tongue they would be able to become as proficient and fluent in that subject as they were in their mother tongue. His violin method has developed as a result of attempting to teach proficiency on the instrument in the same way a child is taught proficiency in speaking its mother tongue.

Dr. Suzuki further clarified, in his 1973 address, five elements that he had observed to be of paramount importance in helping a child acquire the use of its native tongue:

1. The environmental conditions and their influence on the new-born baby as it accustoms itself to the sounds of the mother tongue.

2. Teaching the child by constant repetition to utter its first sound. Usually "Mama, Mama" and so on.

3. Everyday attitude of the parents after the baby starts to talk.

4. Natural progress through daily practice.

5. The skillfulness with which the parents build up enthusiasm in the child, and the happiness the child finds in acquiring its newfound ability.[33]

From these five points, reciprocals can be seen that have become the foundation of the Suzuki violin teaching Method:

1. The use of recordings, cassette-tapes, group lessons, concerts to build a suitable environment of sound to produce fine violin playing.

2. The importance of constant repetition of the repertoire.

3. The importance of the parent and parent-role in Suzuki teaching.

4. Natural progress through daily practice.

5. Parental support to build the student's enthusiasm; letting the child enjoy and glory in her ability—concerts, group lessons, progress attuned to the individual child.

Teaching the violin is only one example of the success of applying the "mother tongue" method of learning to acquiring an ability. The same method has been, and is in the process of being, applied to learning piano, cello, flute, guitar, viola, bass, and harp.

But Dr. Suzuki's concept is even more all-embracing. The application of this method to teaching the highly complex skills of playing musical instruments is proof that it does indeed work and work very well. Dr. Suzuki feels, however, that the mother tongue method should be used in all kinds of education. Of course, it must be adapted to various subject matters but the underlying principles are to Dr. Suzuki *the* education system par excellence.

I learned that the natural method of teaching a child its mother tongue is a marvelous educational process. It fills the child with enthusiasm. It is a natural process in which practice continues from morning to night. The child feels none of the anguish that so often accompanies learning by conventional methods which are applied to other forms of education. What child would refuse to learn its "mother tongue", that is, quit this means of communication because he found the routine dull? Every child in such an environment grows steadily and without mishap toward an involvement in this delightful ability, and responds according to the

47

stimuli supplied it by the parents. With this method, what human abilities might be developed! Superior environment; skill to build up enthusiasm; joy in practice and more practice. Surely, the "mother tongue" method is the most outstanding example of the development of human ability.[34]

In 1948, Dr. Suzuki succeeded in persuading the principal of a primary school in Matsumoto to use the "mother tongue" method of education in the daily routine of one of the four first-grade groups in the school. No one was to be failed and no dropouts were allowed. One child in the class was found to be unable to count up to three and was considered to be retarded. Dr. Suzuki observed, however, that she could speak her native tongue fluently, and persuaded the teacher not to exclude her from school. By the time this child reached the fourth grade with her experimental group of forty, she was performing at the same high level as the rest of the children.

The experimental class was conducted under the following conditions: no homework was assigned, materials were taught in a manner that resulted in their being totally absorbed by the child (that is, the child could use them without conscious effort at recall just as we use our native language); the lessons were performed in an enjoyable atmosphere; and no child was ever made to feel inferior. The initial lessons of the first-graders were considered of vast importance. Just as a child learns its first words very slowly, the beginning was kept to a slow pace. Extremely easy material was chosen for beginning classes. All the children accomplished the tasks required with no mistakes and highest marks. This was teacher Tanaka's start at building confidence and enthusiasm. He made sure that every child understood the material and made no mistakes. Tanaka stressed, trained to and put into practice the theory of no mistakes.

Tanaka recognized the problem of attention span. Some of the children become bored or inattentive after five or six minutes. When this happened, say, in the math lesson, Tanaka would immediately switch to language. When the attention of a child appeared on the wane during the language lesson, Tanaka would switch to another subject. At the end of the year, these youngsters had developed the ability to concentrate on any one subject for forty-five minutes.

Unfortunately, after four years, Principal Himijo, who had given the original permission for the experiment, died, and his successor could not be persuaded to continue the experiment. Dr. Suzuki was most distraught about this and continues to believe in and work toward the adoption of the mother tongue method of education into the educational system. He believes present systems in Japan and elsewhere are destructive to children and are counter-productive, producing failures and dropouts where there need be none.

Dr. Suzuki spoke at the United Nations in October 1968. He asked the United Nations and the countries of the world to unite in establishing and carrying out effective child training and care policies with the utmost speed. He maintained that in every country in the world, countless parents, ignorant of proper child training practices, were rearing miserable twisted personalities. Dr. John Bradshaw is reiterating this message in books and TV series in the 1990s. Bradshaw was nominated for an Emmy for his *Homecoming* series in which he explains how adults can rescue and champion their wounded inner child.

In 1969, Dr. Suzuki visited the Prime Minister of Japan, Minister Sato, and spoke with him about the need for a national policy of child development. "Although he displayed considerable interest," Dr. Suzuki says, "it is sad to relate that nothing came of it. If such a national policy could be carried out in as many countries as possible, I think that in twenty to thirty years a great change in the world would be seen."[35]

To what can we attribute the inaction of the United Nations and individual nations, even in Dr. Suzuki's native Japan? The problem is most possibly political in origin. How could a politician ever get educators to agree on one national policy of education in their own country? How could the many nations reach any agreement?

This is a challenging problem, even though the principles of mother tongue education are not tied to any particular ideology or religion. The violin method has been successfully used in the United States, Europe, Canada, South America, Japan, Korea, Nigeria, and Australia. Students from New Zealand and Malaysia are even now observing the piano method in Matsumoto, with an eye to implementing it in their own countries. If, indeed, the mother tongue method could be used as successfully for general education as it has been in music education, and Dr. Suzuki fervently believes that it can, isn't that enough motivation for an effort to resolve the political problems its implementation could occasion?

There seems to be widespread concern about avoiding an atomic holocaust and de-escalating the arms race. There is also growing international concern about destruction of the environment. There is concern in the United States about the epidemic of addiction. Yet, these concerns do not seem to result in much tangible improvement. Perhaps implementing Dr. Suzuki's educational philosophy would result in the production of an international citizenry that could convert concern into effective action. In Dr. Suzuki's own words, "The love that parents have for their children would be awakened to proper child development through the guidance of trained instructors, and good character and ability would be promoted in every home . . . when one considers the important part for good or evil that . . . future citizen(s) of the world will play, I am unable to understand why the nations forsake such a critical task."[36]

Another reason for the nonimplementation of sound educational policies is, tragically enough, bureaucratic inertia.

There have been voices like Dr. Suzuki's raised in many countries—Maria Montessori in Italy, Ivan Kozal in South America, Kohlberg in the United States—why isn't anything happening? Why do our schools continue in the same non-productive, counter-productive ways?

A reason that seems almost inane, yet may be more pervasive than we think, is perhaps illustrated by this little story. I was deeply immersed in studying curriculum notes at the University of Southern California during June of 1977 in preparation for taking the admissions exam for advancement to candidacy for the Ph.D. in education. I was studying with a colleague also preparing for the exam, who happened to be a high school principal in Southern California. We were discussing various concepts and ideas about improving curriculum planning. "Do you ever have a chance to use any of these ideas in your school?" I asked. "No, I don't have time," he said. "We can barely manage to keep the school running on schedule as it is; there is no way to add such fancy ideas as these to our setup. I'm only studying them so I can pass the exam."

Education seems to have become a self-perpetuating system that operates to perpetuate itself rather than to educate. "We've never done that before," or "it would be too much trouble," or "change doesn't fit into our rules," are unfortunately accepted as sufficient justifications for dismissing ideas that might improve education.

Perhaps it is exactly this that leads to dismissal of Dr. Suzuki's ideas. He has one strong element in his favor that other theorists do not possess, however; he has produced hundreds and thousands of young musicians who can out-perform, at an earlier age, their contemporaries trained by traditional methods. Dr. Suzuki's concertizing with these youngsters brings attention again and again to how well his educational philosophy works. These children are not geniuses (or perhaps every child has greater capacities than we know). They are ordinary children, trained in an extraordinary way, which produces extraordinary results. Why should we not train all children in this way in all subjects and let the world benefit from the extraordinary results? How long will it take for the meaning of that question to penetrate the minds of politicians and bureaucrats and educational administrators? How long must the world wait?

In the spring of 1978, Dr. Suzuki went on tour with 100 Japanese children and 100 American children. The group concertized at the Kennedy Center in Washington, D.C., Carnegie Hall in New York, and Symphony Hall in Atlanta, Georgia. Dr. Suzuki was asked if he would give Suzuki student Amy Carter a lesson while he was in Washington, D.C. He brought writings with him describing his dream of mother tongue education for the world, and his hope of a worldwide movement for the happiness of all children.

Dr. Suzuki has not concentrated solely on applying his theories to music education. In 1948, the same year the experiment with elementary school children was launched in Matsumoto, Dr. Suzuki founded an experimental preschool class that continues to this day at his Talent Education Institute. It was first located in his home where it was given the name "Talent Education Institute." That name was eventually given to the building which now houses both the preprimary school experiment and the instrumental study program.

Children in the preprimary school were and are accepted without any tests. There are sixty children in the class, ranging in age from three to five years. The children are not separated by age because the younger members benefit from the stimulating environment provided by the older children. This is a principle well attested to in the music program, where younger siblings often advance much more rapidly than older siblings, as will be discussed in a later chapter.

The curriculum taught includes Japanese haiku, drawing and calligraphy, English conversation, Japanese, and physical education. Since 1966, the children have been tested for I.Q.

upon graduation. The average I.Q. has been near 160. Here is testimony to the efficaciousness of the mother tongue method of education.

Dr. Suzuki believes that the mother tongue method of education not only develops skills to a high level but actually increases the ability or potential of a child. He uses an analogy to the Alaskan child's development of the ability to withstand cold weather. The stimulation of the frigid Alaskan environment produces an increase in the potential of a child to endure frigid temperatures. So, too, the stimulation of the sound environment produces an increase in the ability of a child to speak the sound of whatever her native tongue may be, or to make beautiful musical sounds. This increase in potential is physiological; Dr. Suzuki feels it is centered physiologically in the brain.

A nonmusical example can be seen in language learning potential. A one- to three-year-old American child who has been in an environment where he or she hears native speakers of Chinese chatting daily can later, as an adult, learn to speak Chinese fluently with no trace of an accent. Other students, who did not hear Chinese spoken when they were young can learn Chinese very well but they do not have that high potential of perfect language acquisition that the person from the richer linguistic environment possesses.

Dr. Suzuki often asks students to play what he calls "games," many of which are aimed at promoting greater automatic control over what is happening. This emphasis on games is what might be called "brain-training." These games are systematically used or played at group lessons. For beginners, the games involve rapid arm motion. Upon signal, each child quickly raises her right hand to touch the top of her head, then lowers it quickly to her side. Later, children may play a piece in segments, one at a time, each taking up immediately where the previous child left off upon signal—usually a handclap. Children are asked to play a piece they know very well while answering questions directed by the teacher. Most recently, I saw Dr.

Suzuki organize a game with a group of young Japanese children who were playing Fiocco's Allegro. He placed a chair in front of the group and upon signal (a handclap), the children ran and touched the chair with their bow hand, then ran back to their places. It was interesting to note that they resumed playing immediately after touching the chair and moved back to place while playing.

The aim is to enable the children to perform several intricate behaviors at the same time. The violin command must be very thorough before a player can carry on a conversation while playing or interrupt and resume her playing without getting lost, especially in a piece so difficult as Fiocco's Allegro. This is indeed brain training. While many adults might find such games incredibly frustrating, the children find them great fun and become very adept at playing them. Developing the ability to converse while playing forces the brain to carry out several very complex behaviors at the same time: speech response, violin playing, recall of the piece being played. Stretching the children's potential to this point is an example of increasing the potential of the brain.

A living example of his own philosophy, Dr. Suzuki at the age of seventy-nine embarked on a new program of mother tongue training. Just as he taught that successful achievement develops greater potential and courage to attempt the difficult, he demonstrated those very qualities in his new endeavor. With financing from an American philanthropist, a new building was constructed at the Talent Institute which Dr. Suzuki uses as a center for mother tongue education from birth to preprimary school age.

Having seen living proof of the success of his philosophy when applied to music education, he desired to extend the benefits of the method to general overall education and development for the very young. He worked primarily with mothers at the outset.

Eventually, he hopes this effort will become the center of a national, then international, policy of "mother tongue" education. As he sees it, the first imperative would be that instructors be stationed throughout a country in the cities, towns, and villages, and that as soon as a birth was registered the instructor would visit the family and teach parents about matters of health and mother tongue principles for developing babies' abilities from the very beginning.

Parents would be taught to do all of this on their own. A deep personal involvement of parent with child would be fostered. The instructor would then visit his territory regularly, give further guidance and assistance to parents, and watch the child's development. Dr. Suzuki feels that if such a system were established and the children of the world were accorded such care, guidance, parental relationship, and sense of their own value and worth, the world would start to change for the better very rapidly.

Some may see this as an overstructuring of a very personal, familial relationship. Yet, how long are we going to leave the very important matter of the rearing of children to chance? How long will we leave parents to struggle with this difficult, challenging, all-important task without giving them the best guidance and counsel available? How long will we leave parents, perhaps themselves twisted personalities as a result of their own faulty education and poor environment, to pass on mindlessly the damage that was inflicted on them by their elders? We do know better ways of fostering emotional, intellectual, and physical development. When are we going to begin using them systematically for the benefit of all? These very questions are reiterated again and again by Dr. John Bradshaw in his books and television series.

Dr. Suzuki doesn't claim to know exactly how the world should go about applying mother tongue principles to overall education. He expects to learn in the process of doing, to find ways of implementing humane learning by working insightfully with each difficulty as it arises.

One problem he has already addressed is the problem of anger. The ability to be angry is not a useful ability, according to Dr. Suzuki, so he decided to let the ability atrophy by non-use. The first year was very difficult, he says, but after ten years he finds it impossible to become angry. Could this be an example of the extinction of an undesirable response through self-initiated counter-conditioning? Certainly the problem of parental anger will have to be dealt with if children are to be educated, without scolding and punishment, as Dr. Suzuki advocates.

The energy and sincerity of this indefatigable man were demonstrated again to me at a Nagono-Ken wide conference on October 25, 1977. At mid-point in the concert, Dr. Suzuki addressed the audience (mostly parents of the 500 children who participated in the concert) very earnestly about education and the importance of the education of their children. Suzuki pianists, violinists, flutists, and cellists participated in the program. The closing number included the audience in the singing of a lovely Japanese song to the accompaniment of many of the previous performers. A beautiful string obligato had been worked out for the piece and was played by memory. When the song was finished, Dr. Suzuki clapped and called for an encore. The audience, with obvious enthusiasm, obliged (an interesting change-about), which emphasized to me the enjoyment of repeating what one has found to be an enjoyable experience. Those who could not sing in Japanese clapped in time.

Finally, Dr. Suzuki had the children repeat after him a threefold saying which has become almost a credo:

> Every child can become educated to a very high level.
> My parents—please educate me (accompanied by a bow
> to the parents in the audience).

Every child can become educated to a very high level. My teachers—please educate me (accompanied by a bow to the teachers at the side of the stage).

Every child can become educated to a very high level. I must be responsible to myself in my education (accompanied by pounding on the child's own chest).

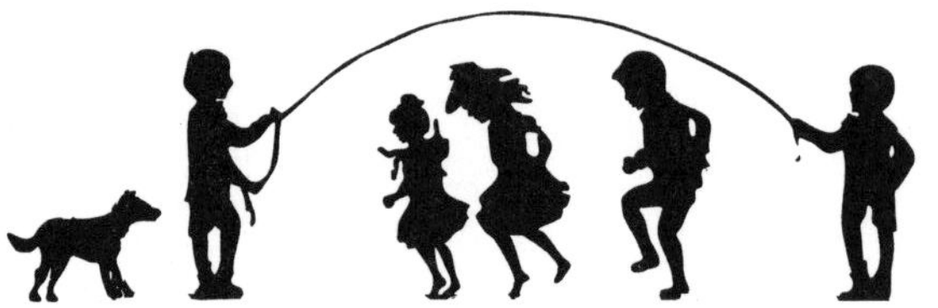

CHAPTER 4

CONDITIONING

The simplest form of animal and human learning is called conditioning. It is a type of learning that is described in terms of changing relationships between stimuli and responses. Classical conditioning involves learning through stimulus substitution. It involves the repeated pairing of two stimuli so that eventually a previously neutral stimulus (one the learner did not react to) comes to evoke the same response as was elicited by the other stimulus. The Russian physiologist I. P. Pavlov first drew attention to this type of conditioning in his experiments with dogs. He found that after repeatedly pairing the sound of a bell and the presentation of food, dogs would salivate only at the sound of the bell. They had so associated the bell with food that the bell could elicit the physiological response of salivation, even when food was not present.[37]

This kind of learning is unconscious. The dog's behavior is changed as a result of his experience of repeated pairing of stimuli. It is important to note that one of the stimuli automatically elicited the response. In the case of the dogs, it was a pleasant stimulus—food.

Edward L. Thorndike maintained, in 1949, that it was the repeated pairing of the pleasant stimulus, food and the bell, that brought about learning or a change in the dog's behavior.[38] Other psychologists (Watson, Guthrie) saw the learning only as a result of contiguity. According to Watson, people are born with a limited number of reflexes and all learning is simply a matter of classical conditioning involving these reflexes.[39]

Thorndike stressed the importance of the *effect* of a response, maintaining that the effect produced learning and that this is an accurate and sufficient explanation for learning.[40] Responses that occur just prior to a satisfying state of affairs will tend to be learned; those which occur prior to an annoying state of affairs will not be learned. The latter part of his theory has been questioned. The first part of the theory was, however, accepted by B.F. Skinner with some modification.[41]

Whereas Thorndike contended that the effect of a response is to strengthen or weaken its connection with the stimulus that preceded it, Skinner maintained that the bond is formed between reward and response, rather than stimulus and response. It is at this point in the evolution of learning theory and theories about conditioning that I believe the Suzuki learning theory and its incredible success are relevant. The results Dr. Suzuki has achieved are a result of using this theory of learning, as I hope to demonstrate in the rest of this chapter.

Dr. Suzuki has additionally developed a fine sequential curriculum, based on behavioral objectives; he has maintained the utmost respect for his students, thus enhancing their self-esteem, and inculcates this into the method; he has used all the ingenuity, creativity, and insight that are essential to fine teaching. These factors contribute, too, to the success of the method. But the solid grounding of all else that is best in the teaching-learning situation on the theory of the bond that is formed between reward and response (Dr. Suzuki calls it the mother tongue method of educating) is the rock on which the rest of the method is built.

Dr. Suzuki's use of Skinner's theory may be an instance of the simultaneous but independent discovery of relationships between phenomenon that are often curiously noted in history. Priestly and Laviosier, for example, isolated oxygen as a separate element at about the same time (during the mid 1700s), although they had no communication whatsoever with each other.[42]

Dr. Suzuki has not studied these ideas of Western physiologists and psychologists. He seems to have arrived at his similar conclusions through his own intuition and experience. Additionally, he has put them to work in a method of music education so successful that the results are not believed. Skeptics charge every kind of fraud. Westerners claim only the Japanese could achieve such results because of their incredible discipline. The Japanese suggest Dr. Suzuki is using American educational concepts. The Americans say he is using Japanese culture. The truth seems to be that he is truly an innovator who put into practice independently created theories of education, which have stayed in the laboratory or educational psychology department at universities in the West.

Just this moment as I am writing in the foyer of the Talent Education Institute in Matsumoto, I have shown Dr. Suzuki the names of Pavlov, Skinner, Thorndike. He has never seen them before! Yet his own theory of learning, the mother tongue theory, is solidly grounded on the importance for learning of the relationship between response to a stimuli and reward, and he has gone on to achieve phenomenal results by applying it.

What are these phenomenal results that I keep speaking of? Basically, they are of two kinds. One is the very high level of mastery to which a large number of students have been educated at a very early age. For example, six-year-olds play the Bach A Minor Violin Concerto by memory accurately, musically and with great happiness and enthusiasm. Eleven-year-olds have played through all ten volumes of the Suzuki repertoire which means they can play, upon request, two Vivaldi concertos (A Minor and G Minor), two Mozart concertos (A major and D major), the Bach A Minor Concerto, and much more. This is truly incredible mastery for such young children. They are not in the traditional sense musical geniuses either, but ordinary Matsumoto children who have had the advantage of being trained under Dr. Suzuki's remarkable program.

It is a hallmark of Dr. Suzuki's method that *every* child can be educated to a very high level of achievement. His students are not tested or screened in any way before being allowed to embark on the program. He takes anyone who comes. In June 1991 in Japan, there were approximately 24,000 Suzuki students (violin, cello, flute, and piano) with 1,600 teachers. In March 1989, 280 violin students completed Book Ten. They had successfully learned Mozart's Concerto No. 4, which is called the Master Course first level. Approximately 5,000 have successfully completed all ten volumes since Dr. Suzuki began teaching in 1946. In March 1989, 208 students graduated the Mozart Rondo and Siciliano (Master Course second level), 162 students graduated Vitali Choconne (Master Course third level) and 116 students graduated the Mendelssohn Concerto (Master Course fourth level).[43]

This kind of result, besides being an astonishing level of mastery at a very early age for a large number of students, is an overall raising of the usual performance quality and level attained by music students. Not every child will go through the ten volumes in three years, but each child does achieve a facility, an enjoyment, and an appreciation of music; if this result has ever been previously proved, I am not aware of it. To be more specific, the average level of achievement after two years of work in a Suzuki program is far greater than anything I have ever seen occur after two years in a typical public school music or study program, or even after two years of private study in the United States. These kinds of results produce enthusiasm, greater motivation to work, and achievement that continues in an ever-widening cycle. The interest and perseverance generated are impressive. They continue to increase, and in geometrical, rather than arithmetic, progression.

While Dr. Suzuki seems to me to be uniquely successful in using what Skinner and others have made theoretical formulations about, others make use of these theories about conditioning as well. *Walden II* is a somewhat horrifying extension by Skinner himself. Dr. Suzuki's effort is, I believe, a much more humane application, applied intuitively, as opposed to the laboratory, mechanistic approach of the behaviorists.

Other psychologists have made attempts to use these same ideas. Dr. James Dobson comes to mind with his *Dare to Discipline*. Referring to the law of reinforcement as a miracle tool, Dobson goes on to suggest means of using it to develop behaviors in their children that parents desire:

> The most magnificent theory ever devised for the control of behavior is called the "Law of Reinforcement" formulated many years ago by the first education psychologist, E.L. Thorndike. It is magnificent because it works. Thorndike's original law has been honed to a sharp edge of effectiveness by the work of B.F. Skinner, who described the conditions under which the principles work most effectively. Stated simply, the law of reinforcement reads: "Behavior which achieves desirable consequences will recur." In other words, if an individual likes what happens as a result of his behavior, he will be inclined to repeat that act.[44]

Dobson recommends using reinforcement to get a child to do such things as brushing teeth regularly, picking up clothes, displaying table manners, and being more responsible with money. Dr. Suzuki uses reinforcement to help his students achieve mastery of the violin. Dobson's evaluation of the law of reinforcement, "It is magnificent because it works,"[45] is impressively demonstrated by Dr. Suzuki's successes in the field of music education.

There is great interest and enthusiasm for the Suzuki Method in the United States in particular. Although I know of efforts to organize Suzuki foundations in Australia, Belgium, Korea, Switzerland, Germany, France, New Zealand, South Africa, England, Malaysia, Canada, the Scandinavian countries, and Nigeria, the most thorough and organized effort I personally know of outside Matsumoto is represented by the Suzuki Association of the Americas.

There are approximately 6,000 registered members of the Association. Members and the board actively work with Dr. Suzuki and his teachers in the further development of the Suzuki Method. For example, members of the Cello Committee for the Association worked in Matsumoto on revision of the cello repertoire with the Suzuki cello teachers. Their aim was to create a cello curriculum that would be the same incremental, sequential developmental backbone of the cello method as the violin curriculum developed by Dr. Suzuki himself.

But I have strayed from the topic of operant conditioning as it emerged from classical conditioning. Let me turn back specifically to operant conditioning and begin with a definition.

Operant conditioning is the type of learning that involves an increase in the probability of a response occurring as a function of reinforcement. Skinner developed the concept of operant conditioning. In his work with white rats he accepts the existence of classical conditioning but considers a larger and more important class of behaviors to be those that are not elicited by any known stimuli but which are simply emitted by the organism. These are labeled operants. The learning bond, Skinner declared, is formed between such emitted responses and reinforcement. Reinforced behaviors will re-occur.[46]

This type of conditioning results in a child learning her mother's native tongue rather than some other language. The human infant is capable of the whole range of sounds made by the human race and emits many of those sounds in her babbling and cooing. But she will learn those that are reinforced by her mother. Hence, Dr. Suzuki's stress on the mother tongue concept of learning. Just as the mother's reinforcement slowly teaches an infant the sounds that produce pleasant situations in her environment, the young violinist is similarly reinforced as she learns the behaviors that produce beautiful violin playing.

Skinner maintains that most significant behaviors fall under the general heading of operant behaviors.[47] According to Guy LeFrancois in his *Psychology for Teaching*, this means that there are relatively few readily observable stimuli that lead to human behavior:

> It also means that reinforcement, or the lack of it, will have a great deal to do with the behavior an individual engages in ... one can hardly overestimate the relevance for teaching of an understanding of the principles of operant learning.[48]

Parents and teachers are powerful dispensers of reinforcement or nonreinforcement to emitted behavior. Dr. Suzuki uses this as a factor in his method of instruction. He motivates children to want to learn to play the violin by first teaching their mothers. The children come to class for at least two months before they are even allowed to touch a violin. This might even be an example of classical conditioning. Seeing their mothers learn to play is a stimulus which elicits the desired response: the wish to learn to play the violin themselves.

Once the children actually begin to learn, operant conditioning is used and a great deal of shaping behavior. Parent and teacher dispense reinforcers with smiles, genuine enjoyment and excitement at the child's progress, bits of candy, stickers, and other special treats at appropriate moments. The result is that the child's behavior of learning the violin is reinforced.

Some of the greatest skill required in Suzuki teaching lies in discerning the right reinforcers for each student. A reinforcer is any stimulus that increases the probability of a response occurring. Hence, if the teacher is working with a beginner to set the habit of holding the violin between chin and shoulder—a side position—rather than the all-too-familiar but incorrect half-front position, great care must be taken to reinforce only that position. Too much attention given to mistakes could be counter-productive.

Since the same situation or stimuli may be highly reinforcing for one person and counter-productive for another, the teacher must be ever alert to what is happening with each student and ready to change strategies at the least indication that the desired behavior is not being reinforced. Herein lies a great deal of the art of Suzuki teaching. It is not a mechanically applied, stereotyped method, that allows not at all for the individual child and the child's reaction's. True, the Suzuki teacher *does* know exactly what behavior she is trying to reinforce. The method of reinforcement is different for each child, however, even with something so basic as the holding of the violin between shoulder and chin.

A very special relationship exists between student and teacher; it involves constant awareness and respect for the student as an individual person with his or her own distinct feelings and reactions. The student responds in turn to this respect for her individuality with cooperation and respect, granted that the student wants to learn to play the instrument. If she doesn't, then the challenge is to motivate the child. She is pleased by this respect for, and attention to, her individual needs and almost invariably responds with cooperation and respect, if not love, for the teacher.

It is most gratifying to a teacher to see how invariable is this human response to respect, even in the smallest child.

Often, little children who have been overwhelmed with demands for instant obedience and conformity by their parents (and are consequently naughty and "difficult" according to their parents) respond so well that it becomes a source of amazement to the parents. They can't understand why the children behave so well at violin lessons and like them so much when every other activity is such a struggle.

When the child achieves rapid success, as every child can using Dr. Suzuki's carefully planned program for development, the child's response is even more gratifying. Although he or she can never seem to please the demanding adults in any other area, the child is actually and demonstrably learning to play the violin, and furthermore, is doing something others seem to think is very "hard." Self-esteem receives an incredible boost. Given the importance that many educators and educational psychologists currently attribute to self-esteem in learning, this could be reason enough in itself to advise learning violin the Suzuki way for every child. Indeed, Dr. Suzuki does incorporate violin playing into his kindergarten program as part of the basic curriculum.

This raising of the self-esteem level is a positive reinforcer of great strength. It motivates the child to continue to learn the violin and results in cooperation and respect for the teacher. With these positive motivations, the endeavor continues to create success after success, and to build a constructive self-perpetuating cycle of great value. The parents usually get caught up in the cycle because they genuinely desire the healthy development of their child, even though the pressures of society to make their children conform at any cost or to rear them "properly" often drive parents into self-defeating cycles of recrimination.

The child's success with the Suzuki Method is a truly positive stroke. Eager to continue the success, the parent will usually cooperate and try to work with the child. The child may perceive for the first time that the parent actually wants her to be happy and the parent's constant demands are not just efforts at denigrating the child and building up the parent's ego. The child perceives that the parent wants to participate in something the child wants to do. The resulting cycle of constructive cooperation can have far-reaching effects on the entire parent-child relationship.

The very young child will need an adult to tune her violin and assist in practicing. Finding a parent ready and willing to help daily can have a very positive effect on the parent-child relationship. The parent is carefully instructed never to threaten, scold, or punish. Parents often report that their little ones beg to practice and want to do so two or three times a day. The practice sessions are very short due to the child's limited attention span (five to fifteen minutes), so usually two or even three practice sessions a day can be managed without strain.

Dr. Suzuki's stance on punishment is unremitting. It is not to be used. This is solidly in line with research that shows punishment is not effective in eliminating behavior, nor in reinforcing it.[49]

> Punishment does not ordinarily illustrate or emphasize desirable behavior, but usually draws attention to undesirable responses; it is often accompanied by highly undesirable emotional side effects and finally it often does not work.[50]

For example, Sears, Maccoby and Levin cite evidence to support the notion that parents who punish their children severely for being aggressive are more likely to have aggressive children.[51]

Dr. Suzuki is one of the few educators I know who insists that no form of punishment be used in conjunction with his instructional program. I have even heard him go so far as to say, "Never scold." Society continues to punish criminals, parents continue to punish children, no matter how much data educators turn up on its contra-indication. The Suzuki approach supports parents and educators in using positive reinforcement *only*.

Dr. Suzuki is absolutely adamant about the non-use of force. He is given to doing works of calligraphy, and most visitors to Matsumoto are presented with one of his works. He was kind enough to write an English translation on the back of my latest gift. The translation may be somewhat lacking in eloquence, but the message is clear: "Never hurt anybody."

Shaping, a technique described by Skinner in 1951 and used experimentally to teach animals complex behavior, is used to teach more and more complicated violin techniques.[52] Skinner's technique involves administering rewards for responses that are not the required terminal response, but which approximate what the experimenter desires. This is called differential reinforcement of successive approximation.

This is very much what the Suzuki teacher does as the child progresses through the curriculum. Dr. Suzuki's insistence that the repertoire be always kept current is a critical part of all this. After a child has learned "Lightly Row," the first piece in the repertoire after "Twinkle Variations," the child goes back and plays "Twinkle Variations." They will be somewhat better as she has acquired more skill in violin playing through learning to play "Lightly Row."

After learning "Song of the Wind" and while learning to play it, the child continues to play "Twinkle Variations" and "Lightly Row" daily. Her execution of both continues to improve.

Each new piece adds one new problem or technique to the child's repertoire of skills. There is no time schedule. The student may take as long or short a time on each piece as is requisite for her to master the necessary skills. William Starr's *The Suzuki Violinist* [53] depicts voluminously the skills learned in each piece for Volumes I through V. Each new piece is a shaping from the known to the unknown. Each old piece is kept in the repertoire so the skills learned will not be forgotten and rudimentarily correct execution can gradually be shaped to fine eloquent execution.

This approach is one of the major elements in Dr. Suzuki's success. I can remember being told by my traditional Western teachers to keep playing all my pieces occasionally, but they never listened to them and there was no emphasis on my keeping memorized pieces always at my fingertips. Of course, they recommended it, but they did not reinforce my doing it; hence, I ceased to do it.

Dr. Suzuki not only recommends it, but regularly hears old pieces. The most advanced teacher-trainee may be asked to play any of the pieces from the ten books of the Suzuki repertoire at any time during a lesson. This is not capricious insistence on rote memorization. Dr. Suzuki builds from his foundations—shapes from his foundations. He uses the earlier repertoire to teach fine points that may be necessary to successful execution of a more difficult piece.

When it becomes necessary to have a bow stroke of equal intensity at all points of the bow, for example, let us say in the first movement of the Handel Sonata in Book Six, Dr. Suzuki may return to the Bach Bouree at the end of Book Three. He will ask the student to play the opening bars of the Bourrée with exactly the same tone quality she used in the lower third of the bow at the tip of the bow. Since the student has long since mastered the Bouree, she has only to try and add this one new skill to her execution. Once she is able to execute the requested behavior, she returns to the Handel Sonata equipped to add the evenness of tone requisite to beautiful execution of its first movement. Dr. Suzuki usually adds that the student should perform the exercise successfully 10,000 times so that the skill will become automatic and will not require conscious effort. Then she can address herself to the other difficulties of the Handel. This is a bit of a joke but the meaning is that it must be repeated as many times as necessary for the learning to take place.

The techniques of shaping used by Dr. Suzuki are not unusual. Positive reinforcement is given for successful approximations of the desired behavior. This reinforcement is in the teacher's smile, a pleasant comment to the student on improvement, commendation for the work behind a successful step. It is a rule that a teacher must always make a positive statement to the student after she has played something for the teacher, no matter how lacking the execution may have been in other ways.

Further reinforcement comes from group lessons and concerts. In fact, I think the *raison d'être* of group lessons is reinforcement. Toba Sensei, one of Dr. Suzuki's most successful Matsumoto teachers, concurs with this. "The children have such fun at group lessons. They enjoy so much playing together and the many games Dr. Suzuki and his teachers have devised for group lessons," she told me. The games always unerringly reinforce some acquisition of proper technique. There are games for proper posture, games for finding higher positions, games for encouraging memorization of the repertoire. Also, there is the sheer pleasure of doing something you can do well with a group who can also do it. Yet, while having fun, the children's ability is continually being developed. I know my own playing improved as a result of playing with the children at group lessons. Part of it is due to making the necessary repetition fun and, hence, ensuring that it actually will take place. Music is never used at the group lessons.

The fabulous Suzuki memory is another phenomenon that occurs quite spontaneously and, for Westerners, almost has to be experienced to be believed. When teachers use and re-use pieces from the early repertoire, children do retain both the ability to play them all well and their memorization of the pieces. Playing the pieces by memory with a group also facilitates memorization. It becomes easy and absolutely dependable. Also, as the pieces gradually become longer, the ability to memorize increases. The student moves almost effortlessly from the total recall of three-line pieces to four-line, six-line, twelve-line pieces, to one movement of a concerto, then three movements of a concerto. Everyone can do it. It has to be seen to be believed, but it absolutely does happen. Six-year olds can play the entire Bach A-Minor Concerto, a university-level work for most in our Western world. With enlightened pedagogical techniques and pedagogy enlightened with love and respect, it is truly amazing what the human brain is capable of and what the children can accomplish.

I would not like to go too far in drawing parallels between Skinner and Dr. Suzuki. Dr. Suzuki arrived at and put into practice the sound pedagogical use of what Skinner later described and termed operant conditioning and shaping. Dr. Suzuki did this independently from and earlier than Skinner. Skinner was putting into a theoretical framework what he saw as regularly observable about learning. Dr. Suzuki observed and put to use the same phenomena.

There is one other striking parallel between Dr. Suzuki and Skinner. This is the emphasis that both men place on environment. "Environment shapes ability," says Dr. Suzuki. "All Japanese children speak Japanese."[54] Skinner contends that man is controlled by his environment but also that man can control that environment.[55]

Dr. Suzuki places great stress on environment from birth and even before birth. The more music a child hears in the womb and from birth the more music he or she can make. Let the child see the mother learning to play the violin, and the child, too, will want to play. Let the child hear and see the pieces that he or she is to learn played well and the child, too, will play them well. Let her be surrounded with others who value and esteem music, and the child too, will value and esteem music. Let the child play the pieces he or she knows so well with others who play them well too, and the child will enjoy them all the more and learn from her immersion in a group who are moving and sounding and concentrating as the child does.

This might be a good place to make the point that Dr. Suzuki's method is not a group method per se as it is often erroneously considered to be. Dr. Suzuki uses group playing as part of his educational strategy. It is a kind of conditioning which leads to improved individual performance. When playing with a group, the individual is immersed in stimuli which brain and body process at their own phenomenal rate, leading to enormous increases in learning. Group playing is never substituted for individual lessons. Suzuki students in Matsumoto always have one or two individual lessons per week. The group playing is an additional learning experience.

The value of group playing can be readily attested to by any teacher who adds group lessons to an ongoing schedule of private lessons. I have personally had this experience. The individual improvement of each student who participates in the group lessons is remarkable.

The reasons for this improvement are not hard to formulate. Operant conditioning and shaping behavior are again at work. Seeing and hearing other students corrected gives an individual the chance to try to improve his or her own playing without being constantly under fire personally. The teacher is ever-present as a model. More about this will be said in the next chapter, "Modeling Behavior."

Group playing is a particular aid to memorization. Individual lapses are not a disaster as the group carries on. A forgotten segment is played in time by the rest of the group and the individual's fingers soon catch up. Seeing the finger and bow movements of the teacher and surrounding players are visual and kinesthetic aids to memorization and the development of correct technique. It is important to note here that this is not all conscious. The great facility of the brain for subliminal perception is utilized.

Great concern is sometimes expressed by professional musicians about Suzuki group playing. They fear that students will be unable to interpret works individually.

This concern has always struck me as ridiculous. Many professionals spend a great deal of time playing in symphonies and playing exactly the same thing as twenty or thirty other violinists in their section and playing it exactly the same way as well. Their capacity for individual interpretation is not harmed.

Dr. Suzuki seeks to teach the violin with any means accessible and is not bound by Western traditions. Once the necessary skill has been acquired by whatever means, then the student can and does go on to individual expression while playing. Indeed, no person *could* ever play a piece exactly the same as someone else even if consciously trying. It is impossible. There will always be individual variations, because each person's body movements are unique. Individual interpretation is the only way anyone *can* play. Each person's performance is always unique and cannot be exactly the same as any other person's performance.

The great concern about Suzuki students reading music well also seems a bit absurd to me. Why teach two very difficult skills concomitantly? It doesn't make pedagogical sense. When this approach is used, the first two years are absolutely paralyzing. No wonder so many students give up in despair and think of music as a hopelessly difficult endeavor. Let technical mastery of the instrument be well along before the student is asked to read music at the same time she is playing. At the very least, let the two skills at first be taught separately and later brought together only when both can be done with relative ease.

It all makes eminent sense, yet there is often a furor over the fact that the children may play the violin for several years before beginning to read. If you start violin at the age of three, you really are not retarded much musically if you don't begin to read until the age of seven. If you are skilled enough to play Vivaldi's A Minor Concerto at seven, (this piece in Volume IV of the repertoire is the point at which Dr. Suzuki suggests the children may be taught to read), what have you lost by not learning to read at the same time you learned to play?

A great factor in the fuss over nonreading of music is that teaching children who don't read is a great deal more demanding of the teacher than the traditional approach. Teaching reading too often takes precedence over teaching the instrument and often can be a mask for the teacher's inadequacy. Teachers who have relied heavily on reading need a good deal of instruction in how to go about teaching by example.

Dr. Suzuki uses many technologies to assist in the teaching. Listening to recordings, playing along with tapes, and watching video tapes all help circumvent the necessity to read. Group lessons are another aid to learning to play without reading. It is the mother tongue method: immersion in a suitable learning environment. Children learn to speak their language before they read it. We learned to speak our native tongues years before we were able to read and write them. We learned by being immersed in an environment of sound, by imitating the sounds we heard and being reinforced when our imitations were meaningful. This is the way Dr. Suzuki teaches violin, and his great success recommends the method. If children can learn to play sooner, advance more quickly, and achieve ultimately a greater degree of skill by learning in this manner, then by all means let us use it. It is a case of the end justifying the means. This may involve some change in sacrosanct Western traditions but there seems to be little real loss.

One legitimate problem that may be raised is what to do with "late" starters, late from a Suzuki point of view. As mentioned earlier, if a child begins at the proper Suzuki age of from two-and-one-half to three, he or she can go through the orderly Suzuki sequence, beginning music reading at age seven or eight when learning Vivaldi, and nothing at all is lost in terms of Western systems. Such a child can play very well at an age when most Western children would just be beginning, and, begins reading music at the same age as is traditional. There is a tremendous gain in ability to play and perfect timeliness in learning to read.

If a teacher wishes to use the Suzuki Method with students who are only beginning to play at the age of seven or eight, some adjustment must be made. The system works as well with older as younger students. Indeed, I have used it to teach teenagers, adults, and senior citizens. All were well satisfied with the approach. A great deal, of course, depends on how much time and effort the older student is willing and able to put into violin. I had one student in his late teens who started at sixteen and went through four Suzuki volumes in two years. He chose to learn strict Matsumoto style, reading very little if at all. He was doing it for the discipline just as some youngsters do Tae Kwan Do.

A senior citizen who had played a bit as a youngster desired to play in a symphony. He spent a year doing the method while reviewing reading separately but at the same time. Within nine months he had been accepted into the second violin section of a local symphony.

Another adult student was a lawyer who had a hankering to play country fiddle and bluegrass. She had never played the violin before. She knew how to read music from piano lessons as a child. After a year of strict Suzuki learning she went off to a seminar in West Virginia to learn the fiddle tunes. She had developed a nice Suzuki memory and more than sufficient technique to handle most challenges of fiddle playing. She also developed an interest in classical violin and continued on with the Suzuki method as well as her bluegrass music.

The problem of the seven-or eight-year-old western student who is just beginning is that, if learning to read is held off for four years, he or she may not be able to play in orchestras and other groups that are available. The best solution here is to teach reading concomitantly. That is, teach the Suzuki materials as usual by example, listening, group playing, playing with tapes. No reading should be introduced with this part of the learning. Concurrently, however, note-reading of materials other than the Suzuki curriculum can be taught. There are many methods for teaching reading available at most music stores and any of these can be used.

One of the most common-sense reasons for not teaching reading while playing is that it militates against proper position. The immediate response of a student who has stand and music placed in front of him or her is to turn the eyes and face toward the music, thus destroying the carefully taught nose, strings, elbow, foot position. When the student does begin to play in orchestra, Starr recommends that Dr. Suzuki's formula for posture for the beginner—nose, string, elbow, foot—be expanded to "nose, string elbow, foot, music, conductor." [56]

In this concomitant teaching of reading, the Suzuki principle of teaching a little bit at a time and making sure that it is thoroughly mastered should be followed. The student should know the symbols of musical notation before actually using them. After learning the symbols, the child should be given very simple music to actually read and play at the same time. Problems of rhythmic notation and pitch notation should be presented separately at first. Then, the teacher should repeat a limited vocabulary of symbols with many variations. New problems should not be added too quickly, or the student will not be able to recognize the symbols automatically.

One final, cogent reason for not teaching the actual reading of each piece as it is learned—it may impair development of the fine Suzuki memory which is an immeasurable bonus of the Suzuki Method. Many very fine Western performers are troubled in their musical development by what they bemoan as their inability to memorize. This is an impossibility for the authentically trained Suzuki violinist, who memorizes almost automatically; anyone trained in the Suzuki way will acquire this ability. Part of it comes from repetition; another part comes from the sensitivity of the student's listening behavior.

Music to the Suzuki student is sound, not a system of notation. Notation has never stood between the comprehension of sound and the ability to produce or reproduce sound. Thus the student is freer, closer to music. Once having learned a piece, it is his or hers. All that is needed is a violin on which to perform it; dragging a stand and music is not necessary. Again, the analogy to language is apropos. Little children do not rush about clutching dictionaries and grammar books as they learn to speak their language. They listen, their brain records, they produce sound, they are reinforced for reproducing certain sounds, and their language becomes a part of them. So, too, the Suzuki violinists' repertoire becomes a part of them.

In conclusion, I must admit that I have pondered at times just how much of Suzuki training could be considered classical conditioning as opposed to operant conditioning. Does the reinforcement of love and praise elicit the child's development on the violin? Very possibly this is so and therefore would be called classical conditioning. On the other hand, once the violin-playing behaviors have been elicited and the child begins emitting them independently, the shaping of those behaviors begins. They are patiently and lovingly shaped until the child is capable of fine, sensitive, beautiful execution of music on the violin.

It might be said that classical conditioning provides the basic motivation while operant conditioning and the shaping of behaviors give the pedagogical mechanism used to achieve the high degree of skill necessary to fine violin playing. Whatever the relationship, the result is undeniably impressive. It is a testimony to what the loving application of conditioning can achieve.

CHAPTER 5

MODELING BEHAVIOR

One of the wellsprings of the success of the Suzuki Method is the use it makes of the teacher, parent, siblings, and other students as models of behaviors that the young violinist needs to acquire. This goes back to Dr. Suzuki's development of his teaching method from watching the way a young child acquires its native language. Much of the mother tongue learning pattern is a learning that derives from imitation of a loved and admired model.

This kind of learning has been theoretically discussed by Bandura and Walters [57] and Bandura. [58] It is based largely on operant conditioning, which was discussed in Chapter Four. The concept of modeling behavior, however, goes beyond operant conditioning. The difference lies in the source of the reinforcement.

Bandura and Walter's theory asserts that much human learning is a function of observing the behavior of others. We learn to imitate through being reinforced for doing so. Continued reinforcement maintains imitative behavior. The reinforcement comes from three sources.

1. Direct reinforcement of the learner by models.

2. The consequences of the behavior itself.

3. Vicarious reinforcement: the learner's assumption that models are deriving some pleasure from their behavior because otherwise they wouldn't be engaging in it.[59]

The effect of reward/punishment of models has been seen to be transferred vicariously to learners, too.[60]

Dr. Suzuki makes use of all these types of reinforcement in his mother tongue pattern of learning. The teacher's praise of and pleasure at the student's achievement are examples of the first type of reinforcement. Also, Dr. Suzuki's practice of first teaching the mother to play the songs the child will learn and then using her as the teacher in the home continues the possibility of the modeling effect and direct reinforcement from an admired model every day. Group lessons further widen the possibilities for modeling. The teacher performs with the children, providing an exemplary model. Other students on all sides offer a rich environment for almost unconscious learning of bowing and finger patterns through modeling behavior. Concerts of twenty, fifty, one hundred, one thousand performers extend the possibilities even further. Performances and concerts are always a learning experience in the Suzuki system, not an occasion for showing oneself off or for competition.

The consequences of learning the modeled behaviors are manifold. The child experiences the physiological pleasure of being able to produce a sound sequence that he or she considers beautiful and that family and others consider beautiful. The physical activity in itself becomes pleasurable and creates the desire to be able to produce another and another such sequence, by doing as the teacher does and emulating sounds heard on recordings. Becoming more skilled, the child can not only reproduce the sequence but also becomes able to express something that is uniquely individual. This is so pleasurable that the child seeks to do it again and again. Different pieces enable children to express different things within themselves. The enthusiastic audience that a Suzuki program always produces becomes strongly reinforcing as it is the expression of the student's very being that is received and responded to by these significant others.

Vicarious reinforcement from observing models is also abundantly available in a Suzuki program. Students observe the joy and enthusiasm with which one child's achievement is greeted by parents, teacher, and audiences. They anticipate similar reinforcement will be theirs if they can achieve the same success. At group lessons, students see other students praised for certain behaviors which they then strive to imitate, and corrected for other behaviors which they then try to avoid. This avoidance of behaviors that are corrected in other students is an example of using the inhibitory effect of modeling behavior. The many home concerts and after-concert parties are also part of the effort to make performance a celebrated, joyous occasion that will motivate students to pursue their studies diligently.

Bandura and Walters show in their laboratory experiments how a novel, aggressive response can be elicited from children as a result of exposing them to aggressive actions of models. The learning of a language is also an example of modeling, according to them. In reference to language learning, the model can be a person, tape, book, or record; it makes no difference because the latter three are symbolic models. The term "model" may refer to an actual person whose behavior serves as a stimulus for an observer's response, or it may refer to symbolic models, such as books, tapes, records. Considering this expanded definition of a model, the extent to which the Suzuki Method uses the modeling effect becomes even more apparent.

The chapter on Learning Machine Technology documents this usage in depth. Briefly, the child is immersed in a piece before attempting to learn to play it; it is played on tapes, by the teacher, by other students; practice is accompanied by cassette tapes that have the violin part dubbed softly in the background. In Japan, the student may play with the "Practice With Me" tape each day, which includes playing short segments of the piece to be learned with Dr. Suzuki's own encouragement to try and imitate each segment well before putting the whole piece together.

Dr. Suzuki's practice of having students observe other students' lessons is another use of this modeling effect. Dr. Suzuki encourages this practice at all levels. With lessons scheduled at fifteen minute intervals (but which last as long as the students' attention span sometimes only five minutes for a two-and-one-half-year-old) Young students arrive in time to observe one or two earlier lessons. The foreign *Kenkyusei's* lessons are scheduled on one afternoon in Dr. Suzuki's studio, usually from 1:30. He teaches in English on this afternoon and usually all the *Kenkyusei* (teacher trainees) will be present from 1:30 for the entire afternoon of lessons. Thus, students learn by observing and modeling. The inhibitory effect (suppression of a behavior as a result of seeing a model corrected for it) helps rapid learning to take place, as well as the modeling effect of seeing others emit desired behaviors and seeing them be reinforced for correct behaviors. This use of the modeling and inhibitory effects is one of the factors that account for the accelerated rate of development that occurs when the Suzuki Method of learning is used.

Student observation of the lessons of others not only uses the modeling effect but the effect of reinforcing only a single model also is transmitted to the observer. Thus, vicarious reinforcement is occurring here too.

Another effect of the modeling behavior is termed by Bandura and Walters the "eliciting effect." This is the eliciting of responses that do not precisely match those of the model but are related to the model's behavior. The many performances and concerts encouraged by Dr. Suzuki produce this effect. Students are stimulated to learn their particular piece better, or try to improve their tone quality or bowing technique, as a result of seeing a model perform a different piece exquisitely well, or with a particularly luscious tonal quality, or with a dash and verve that are perceived to be related to a solid bow technique. On these occasions, the models are not copied but elicit related responses in the observers.

While this chapter is short, its brevity is not an indication of lack of importance. The Suzuki method makes most effective use of the learning that can occur through modeling behavior. Its use of teachers, video and audio tapes, recordings, compact discs, group lessons, home concerts, performances, parents as teachers, is ingenious in eliciting the maximum gain from the human capacity to learn through modeling behavior.

I might add this is a much more pleasant way of learning than traditional methods, that involve long hours of solitary practice, struggling not only with a new and difficult instrument but also an almost indecipherable set of strange musical symbols, all at the same time. It is much more enjoyable to find that violin study is an experience that involves cooperation with and reinforcement from many significant others.

Long hours of practice may eventually become part of the entire effort too, but they come from the student's eagerness to pursue this pleasant, rewarding and challenging endeavor. They are not unpleasant, lonely hours of struggling that all too often are spent with the traditional approach. The great surge of interest in violin playing occasioned by Dr. Suzuki and the perseverance of Suzuki students to high levels of mastery attest to the pleasantness, as well as the effectiveness, of the use of modeling behavior.

Dr. Suzuki's curriculum with its use of pleasant folk music and lovely classical selections, rather than ugly, arduous, boring exercises, contributes mightily to this pleasantness also.

Dr. Suzuki has written some Etudes but they are tuneful and interspersed sparsely throughout the curriculum. His book of position etudes is based on the familiar Perpetual Motion of Book I. Playing familiar folk and classical selections is also a part of the modeling paradigm. It is a joy to be able to play familiar and well-loved models.

CHAPTER 6

CURRICULUM AND PROGRAMMED INSTRUCTION

Dr. Suzuki spent ten years developing the curriculum presented in his ten volumes for violin. He developed the manuals one by one, piece by piece, on a trial and error basis. He kept what worked well and discarded what did not. This work he did in the 1920s and 1930s. The curriculum is now published by Zen-On in Japan. Summy-Birchard is the sole publisher for the world except Japan.

The volumes move progressively. Each new piece teaches one or two new skills. The developmental sequence is very carefully explained in Starr's *The Suzuki Violinist*. This careful sequence is another cornerstone of the success of the Suzuki Method. It bears similarities to what educationists in the West have termed "programmed instruction."

Programmed instruction is defined by educational psychologists as an instructional procedure that makes use of the systematic presentation of information in small steps, usually in the form of a textbook or employing some other device. The computer industry is currently using this approach in much educational software. Programs typically require the learner to make responses and provide immediate knowledge of results.

Dr. Suzuki most certainly grounds his method on proceeding systematically in small steps. His painstakingly developed curriculum is based on this. His teachers are carefully trained to be aware of the important new skill that is being developed in each piece. This is accomplished through oral tradition among the teachers, through Dr. Suzuki's Japanese tape series on Books I-IV, in which he carefully explains the important points in each piece (this was made for and is directed to the practicing child but is also an invaluable aid for teachers). A third source of such information is the publications of the Suzuki associations, conventions, and societies. The finest explication that I know of in English is Starr's *The Suzuki Violinist*. The teacher training institutes and teacher training programs of the Suzuki Association of the Americas also provide this vital training.

Examples of this careful sequence abound in the repertoire. In Book I there are two new behaviors that are to be learned in the third piece in the book, "Song of the Wind," the use of the third finger on the A and E strings consecutively, and the use of consecutive down-bows. These are the only new patterns that occur in the piece. Dr. Suzuki states that these two new patterns are the main challenges of the piece.

The next piece, "Go Tell Aunt Rhody," has no new finger patterns at all. This piece introduces a longer bow stroke for the first time and this new bowing style is the central point of the piece. "Come Little Children," the next piece in the book, adds no new finger patterns. The only new problem is playing two up-bows in succession.

In addition to this incremental development of new skills with each new piece in the curriculum, Dr. Suzuki at lessons often uses old pieces to teach a new skill. Much of the development of bow technique is taught in this fashion. The principle of reinforcement of previous learning is used here too. Bow strokes of different lengths are required as the student reviews selections.

Vibrato, tone production, and position studies are taught, using early, easy pieces. This method of teaching various bow strokes and positions is certainly preferable, in my opinion, to struggling through the exhaustive and exhausting method books often used in the Western traditional approach to violin. Dr. Suzuki approaches these challenges using familiar melodies that the student already knows thoroughly. The student has to pay conscious attention only to adding the new skill. Transposing is learned effortlessly as a result of this approach also; playing in second or third or whatever position means playing in a different key as well.

And so it goes, on and on and back and forth, through ten volumes of carefully selected curriculum materials. Goals are already identified for each piece and in the teacher's mind. Completion of the goals is definable in terms of observable new behaviors. These new behaviors or performance objectives can be praised and reinforced as they are accomplished. It is a very sensible and educationally sound manner of proceeding. Reams have been written about the importance of stating educational goals in behavioral terms and Dr. Suzuki certainly has accomplished that. The success of his method is a testimony to those who put credence in the behavioral objectives approach.

The teacher gives immediate positive feedback to the student on the success of efforts. Undesired behaviors are ignored. Parents are also trained to do this. The steps are small and sequential enough that usually they are achieved quite easily. Dr. Suzuki makes a point of not hurrying the children through each step. They enjoy doing what they *can* do and should be allowed to savor each achievement before going on to the next one.

Ambitious parents can present a problem here; it may be necessary to educate them. It is of primary importance to the overall aims of Suzuki violin that the children be allowed to enjoy their achievements. Production of prodigies is not an aim of the method. If the parents begin pushing the speed with which the child moves, he or she may lose interest altogether in the undertaking. On the other hand, the child communicates very clearly to the teacher when he or she is ready to move on and that is exactly when it should be done. No sooner and no later. The truly incredible achievement of children when this method is followed is usually more than enough to satisfy most parents.

Allowing the student to progress at his or her own rate is one of the advantages most often claimed for programmed instruction in other learning endeavors. There is a distinct difference in the Suzuki Method from many programmed instruction sequences in that it is definitely not auto-instructional. The teacher is collaborating and feeding the information necessary to acquiring new behaviors to the student at all times. Yet the student-teacher relationship is a very special one in Suzuki violin and the very basic respect that the teacher always accords the pupil does make learning, in some sense, student-centered. There is a kind of cooperation between student and teacher that keeps the teacher's ego out of the relationship.

In terms of operant conditioning, Dr. Suzuki's carefully constructed program of violin instruction leads the student to emit desired behaviors and provides for immediate reinforcement of desired achievements. If students have been conditioned properly, it is almost uncanny how rapidly they can acquire a totally new behavior. Proper conditioning would include (1) listening to a new piece many times before ever attempting to play it, (2) seeing and hearing the teacher play the new piece before ever attempting it, (3) seeing and hearing other students play the piece at group lessons before ever attempting it.

These conditions are often at optimum when a younger brother or sister begins Suzuki lessons, at, say, age three after an elder brother or sister, age six, has been studying for three years. The speed with which the younger child learns to play may lead the rest of the family to conclude that he or she is a veritable genius, much to the chagrin of the elder sibling. The frequency with which this occurs, however, leads me to suspect it is due to the excellent conditioning and environment the younger sibling has had. He or she has heard the records from infancy; has always seen and heard someone nearby playing the violin; indeed, may think everyone in the world plays the violin. It may seem like brushing one's teeth or eating—something that everybody does. This child is exquisitely prepared to achieve a very great deal on the violin. Dr. Suzuki comments on this greater achievement of younger siblings as a perfect example of the importance of environment in education. Optimum environment produces optimum results.

I don't wish to leave the impression that Dr. Suzuki's curriculum is a rigid, unchanging sort of thing. The sequence and pieces used to teach the skills necessary to fine violin playing are comparatively fixed. This is because they work so well (no one considers them divinely inspired, however), and because the great importance of repetition necessitates a stable repertoire. This stable repertoire makes it possible to use earlier pieces as an aid to acquiring a difficult new skill. The old piece is so much a part of the student that it is automatic. He or she can add the new skill (drawing full and half bow strokes, for example, in "Go Tell Aunt Rhody"), being able to concentrate intensely on only this new skill since the rest of what must be done is automatic. It is a very efficient way to acquire new and increasingly complex skills.

Right brain, left brain synchronization is important here also. The importance of repetition is illustrated again. Repetition makes the piece automatic. The automaticness of the piece makes it an efficient tool for learning new skills. As the student moves through the sequence, an ever-widening base for the acquisition of more and more difficult skills becomes automatic. The learning potential becomes greater and greater.

The student's actual ability is increasing (her potential is increasing), as Dr. Suzuki so often says.

The stable sequence and material is important but new approaches are constantly being developed also. In Matsumoto, there is a teachers' meeting every Friday afternoon where new ideas, insights, games, and strategies for teaching are exchanged and discussed. Dr. Suzuki encourages these teachers' innovations and insights and gratefully acknowledges his indebtedness to them in the struggle to find ways to present the curriculum to children in the clearest and easiest manner possible. Each May, all Suzuki teachers in Japan meet for a five-day conference. The teachers give presentations of their new ideas, study together, and have practical training sessions. Every other year, an international conference is held with the same aims.

Each time I visit Matsumoto I find Dr. Suzuki using some new ploy or device for helping teacher trainees acquire the art of violin playing as an almost integral part of themselves. On this visit I found him asking people to try to play the Handel Chorus (from Volume II of the repertoire) with closed eyes, still keeping their bows always on the Kreisler Highway, his term for the horizontal placement of the bow on the strings which renders optimum tone quality. This is no mean feat. Other students were to clap only if the attempt was successful. Not many succeeded but there was a good deal of laughter, particularly at the teachers' Friday afternoon conference. Here, too, is an example of the philosophy of adding difficulty after difficulty to the execution of a relatively easy and automatic piece.

So the curriculum is not a mechanical, rote, unchanging sort of thing. Dr. Suzuki encourages teachers to use their individual creativity and ingenuity to provide a successful interaction between the student and the curriculum. The curriculum is the supporting backbone of the method. The teacher progresses through it with each student and moves back and forth teaching difficult skills with early pieces as the teacher's pedagogical artistry and intuition suggests.

CHAPTER 7

USE OF LEARNING MACHINE TECHNOLOGY

Dr. Suzuki makes use of many technological devices to aid the teaching and learning of violin. Among the devices in use in Matsumoto are a closed-circuit TV system, an electronic pitch device for tuning, tape decks in every teaching room for taping and playing back recordings, and tape recorders with adjustable pitch (a device for slowing or speeding the movement of the tape). Devices used at home by the students are their lesson tapes, tapes of piano accompaniments, and recordings of the repertoire. In Japan, each of the ten Suzuki books originally came with a recording of its contents so that the pupil could listen to each new piece before, during, and after learning it. Now there are companion cassette tapes and compact discs of the repertoire available as well.

One of the reasons for the success of Dr. Suzuki's method is his ingenious use of such technological devices. An important point to be made in regard to this usage, however, is its total subservience to the overall goal of teaching mastery of the violin. The technology is never an end in itself but a means to an end. With that important distinction kept in mind, the sky is the limit. Anything that works or helps will be used.

When a parent purchases Volume I of the Suzuki manuals, the companion cassette or recording is as important as the music. The child is to begin listening to the tape or record immediately and is to listen to it every day, at least to the piece that is currently being learned. Each succeeding volume comes with a companion cassette or recording and the same principle applies. Dr. Suzuki stresses again and again the importance of this listening. He insists the students will not make rapid or satisfactory progress unless they listen daily to the tape or recording. This is in line with his belief in the importance of the total environment in encouraging and fostering learning, an environment of sound in this case. Also, the daily listening begins, and later enhances, the acquisition of each piece as an automatic and integral part of the student's very being.

Dr. Suzuki writes in a 1977 Talent Education bulletin, "I consider the invention of the cassette tape recorder as a revolutionary tool for music education."[61] Dr. Suzuki utilizes cassette tapes in several ways.

He has made a sequence of tapes called *Practice With Me*. The purpose of these tapes is to encourage and make enjoyable daily practicing. Dr. Suzuki talks the young child through a practice sequence, making jokes, dispensing Zen-like aphorisms in his own inimitable fashion. Each piece is worked in segments and then put together. Then, there is piano accompaniment with which to play the piece. These tapes have been widely welcomed in Japan because they spare the mother much trouble, while the children find it makes their practicing very enjoyable. These tapes have been made for Volumes I-IV.

Another series of tapes used with Suzuki instruction are the accompaniment tapes. Piano accompaniment for each piece is included with an A tone for initial tuning and rhythmic beats at the start of each piece to indicate tempo. The violin part is very softly dubbed in the background with the sound of the accompaniment being prominent. These tapes encourage sensitive musical renditions: dynamics, phrasing, and tempo changes are used to enhance the performance. Correct musical tempo is set.

The accompaniment tapes are also used to help judge when a child is ready to go on to the next piece. If the student can play satisfactorily with the tape, she is allowed to go on to the next piece. The matter of tempo is often a difficulty. American students in particular tend to learn the pieces adequately but can play them only very slowly. This is usually an indication that there hasn't been enough listening or repetition of the piece. The piece has not yet become an automatic, integral part of the student. Dr. Suzuki insists that a student should be able to play a piece at "Matsumoto Tempo" and with "international intonation" before beginning a new piece. The piece should be learned to mastery. This is one of the major differences between traditional methods and the Suzuki approach. Traditional teaching often moves on when the student gets a piece "right." Suzuki students move on when they can't get it wrong.

This is not a punitive measure; it is a reflection of the importance of really mastering the skills requisite for a piece before adding new problems. Dr. Suzuki feels it is a great mistake to push youngsters into new difficulties before they can handle the present task. In fact, this is one of the great weaknesses he sees in school curricula. Blind adherence to a set schedule and curriculum can only be harmful to the student. Students must be allowed to move at their own pace, however fast or slow that may be. When children are not being scolded, coerced, and forced to tackle tasks that are too difficult for them it is amazing just how fast they will move. The movement is to be gauged to the student, however, and not to parents' ambitions, school schedules, or any other thing. As Dr. John Bradshaw put it in his PBS series *Homecoming*: school is the only place where success is a function of time rather than accomplishment of the task.[62]

Another utilization of cassettes made by Dr. Suzuki is the taping of each lesson. Students are expected to attend the lesson with their own tape recorder so that they can tape the lesson and then use the tape during their practice at home. This enables the student to work at home on the points the teacher stressed during the lesson. It helps to make home practice a useful, efficacious endeavor and avoids the repetition of mistakes during practice.

A final use of tapes in Japan is the presentation of graduation tapes. Gossec Govatte (Volume I), Bach Bourrée (Volume III), Vivaldi Concerto in G Minor, first movement (Volume V); Bach Concerto in A-Minor, all movements (Volume VI), are designated as graduation pieces. The student submits a tape of her graduation piece to Dr. Suzuki. There is a graduation tape accompaniment series for the first four graduation pieces. These ensure proper tempo and encourage musical interpretation. Dr. Suzuki listens to the student, then returns the tape with a graduation certificate and a few personal words of praise and encouragement.

This is an effort aimed primarily at motivation and is extraordinarily effective. Dr. Suzuki's daily schedule includes listening to tapes every morning, beginning at 3:00 a.m. This is a part of his fifteen-hours-a-day work schedule; he requires only six hours of sleep. In 1976, he listened to 6,000 graduation tapes from his Japanese students.

The system is an effective motivating device in many ways. It stimulates students to work hard on their particular graduation piece in order to complete it satisfactorily and turn in the tape. It stimulates teachers' efforts to develop a very high level of performance on the tape. I was fortunate enough to participate in this graduation program from my studio in Korea. Dr. Suzuki's comments to my students were unerringly accurate in terms of technical adjustments that may have been required. Although he had never seen the students play, he could discern by their sound if an elbow needed to be raised or lowered, a finger curved, or a bow placed closer to the bridge. This was very inspiring to me as a teacher.

No students who submit tapes fail to graduate. This is in line with Dr. Suzuki's overall educational philosophy of no failure and no dropouts in education. Graduation ceremonies are held locally in each classroom all over Japan. The certificates are given to the children by their own teachers and then a graduation concert takes place. In the United States, students give graduation recitals followed by parties and celebrations.

Dr. Suzuki says of the system of graduation tapes: "For the children to have a goal that can be reached through their own efforts is a great joy and brings out very fruitful results. I hope that this graduation system will be introduced to countries all over the world." This system is another of the rewards that can be built into the program to motivate students.

Tape recorders that include a device for slowing or hastening the speed of the tape are particularly useful for home practice. If a student's violin is tuned to A at 440 vibrations per second and the accompaniment tape is higher or lower in pitch, the machine can be adjusted to the pitch of the violin. Otherwise, it is impossible to practice unless the violin is re-tuned, which can be a time-consuming effort. It is preferable for the children to hear A regularly at 440 anyway, so this contrivance is very useful. They can easily be taught perfect pitch beginning with this 440 A.

Another learning machine used in Matsumoto is a closed-circuit TV system located in Dr. Suzuki's studio. He uses it for instantaneous viewing by the student while the two of them are playing or working on a particular problem or technique together. The underlying reason for utilization of this device is the use Dr. Suzuki makes of modeling behavior as a pedagogical technique. This has been discussed in full detail in Chapter Five. The closed-circuit TV greatly enhances the modeling that can be done; it makes it possible for the student to play and at the same time observe what Dr. Suzuki is doing and how close what he or she is doing comes to approximating the movement Dr. Suzuki is making.

Perhaps the old adage, "One picture is worth a thousand words," can best convey how helpful the TV is in showing students what is lacking in their movements as compared to what the desired movement is. The student can attempt to adjust and note immediately if their change is closer and how much closer to the desired behavior. Operant conditioning and shaping behavior are at work here; the student can be the judge of the success of their successive approximations of the desired behavior. The instant feedback is another valuable pedagogical plus. Inappropriate behaviors can be dissolved this way and appropriate behaviors shaped up with a minimum of effort and discussion.

A different kind of help from technology is utilized by Dr. Suzuki in the constructing of violins of various sizes to suit his many young students of varied ages. The smallest violin I have seen used in Matsumoto is a 1/16th-size instrument. This is the size required for the smallest beginner. A Suzuki teacher in the Washington, D.C. area recently had a 1/32nd-size instrument made for her two-year-old to begin lessons. These are now available in music stores in the area.

Dr. Suzuki first tried teaching tiny youngsters in Tokyo in the late 1920s. The immediate problem, of course, was finding instruments suitable in size for three-year-olds. Mr. Suzuki's family owned the largest violin factory in Japan. The factory was located in Nagoya and Mr. Suzuki asked his brother if he could make violins small enough for his tiny pupils. That is how the first small violin came into being. The family was financially ruined in the 1929 stock market crash; they had just begun to rebuild when World War II hit and the factory was bombed. Only a small portion was left but after a period of terrible deprivation, handmade violins again began to be made in Nagoya following the war.

Into this situation came Dr. Suzuki's continuing requests for small violins. The problem was manifold, however, as a three-year-old rapidly outgrows his 1/16th-size violin and, accordingly, 1/10th- and 1/8th-size violins were developed for the growing violinists. One-quarter size violins had been made before in Germany and Italy, as had 1/2- and 3/4-sizes.

Proper sizing is a very crucial factor if the children are to develop a fine violin technique. When the violin becomes too small, proper movement is impeded and the fingers become too large to play in tune on tiny instruments. Bowing is also impaired as the natural positioning grows further and further away from the Kreisler Highway in the direction of the fingerboard. Forcing the bow back to the Kreisler Highway puts the bow elbow in a strained position which is inimical to the production of the beautiful sound Dr. Suzuki desires.

Instruments that are too large present different difficulties. The proper position of the left arm elbow and fingers cannot be attained if the student is stretching to reach first position. The bow is too long and unwieldy to manage with any ease and the bow elbow may have to be pulled awkwardly forward in order to be positioned on the Kreisler Highway.

Small violins now being made in the U.S., Japan, Korea and Germany solve these problems. Machine-made instruments are available in abundance and, as the importance of tone becomes paramount, more expensive hand-made instruments are also available. The innovation of Dr. Suzuki that made this all possible should not be overlooked, however. His belief that tiny children could learn to play the violin and his arranging to have instruments as small as 1/16th-, 1/10th- and 1/8th-size constructed, made possible what before was considered impossible or just wasn't considered. Youngsters aged two to six now can begin learning the violin. Before Dr. Suzuki there were no instruments small enough for them to even make the attempt.

Another teaching technique used by Dr. Suzuki is the application of tapes to the bow and fingerboard to help students learn various bow-strokes and finger positions. I can recall feeling terribly ashamed at a recital in which I played, in the fifth grade, because my teacher was forced at the last moment to put a bit of tape on the violin fingerboard to indicate a particular high note that I never could seem to manage to play in tune. I felt I had let down the whole Western tradition of music and was doing a terribly reprehensible thing.

Dr. Suzuki has no such compunction and that is a fortunate thing indeed for his students. With three bits of tape applied to the violin fingerboard to indicate the positioning of fingers on the A and E string, a three-year old can be taught fairly easily to play "Twinkle." In a very short time, the child will know as if by radar just where those fingers go and will be able to play without the tapes. This first finger pattern becomes known as the Twinkle Pattern, or Finger Pattern One. It is then possible to move the tapes and teach another finger pattern.

Dr. Suzuki has used careful synchronization of the violin tapes and curriculum with this technique. All but the last five pieces of Volume I are played in the Twinkle Finger Pattern—the pattern for the key of A Major which was chosen by Dr. Suzuki because it requires the same pattern on the A string as the E string. The student can use this position automatically and easily by the time the twelve first pieces in Volume I have been mastered. It is with the thirteenth piece, "Etude," that a new finger pattern, or Finger Pattern #2, is learned. "Etude" is written in the key of G so that it utilizes the new finger pattern on the A and E strings, but retains the first finger pattern on the D and G strings. Thus, the new is added but the old is reinforced.

In summary, then, it can be seen that Dr. Suzuki has been a great innovator in the application of various technologies to the teaching of the violin. He has introduced the use of cellophane tapes to teach bow strokes and finger patterns. This is not a new device but certainly Dr. Suzuki has innovated in using it so extensively and so systematically. He has introduced the use of tiny instruments to fit tiny children; and the use of the cassette tape in four innovative ways: (1) to practice, (2) to tape lessons, (3) to record and listen to one's own sound, and (4) to continuously listen to each piece to provide the proper sound environment for rapid learning. These innovations are part and parcel of his method. The use of closed-circuit TV, special kinds of tape recorders, and electronic pitch devices, are part of the optimum learning situation in Matsumoto, but are not so requisite for using the Suzuki Method as are the recordings, small-size violins, cello-tape technology and work with cassettes recordings and compact discs.

In writing about these innovations in retrospect, they seem almost obvious, logical applications of technology to the learning of violin by small children. Hindsight is twenty/twenty. We are tempted to say, why didn't someone think of this before? The same is easily said of many great discoveries after they have been pointed out to us by someone with enough foresight, imagination, and individuality to make these innovative efforts on their own. Perhaps this is the essence of genius: to be able to see and apply what really should be perfectly obvious but is not seen by anyone else. Dr. Suzuki certainly has been an innovative genius in his application of these various technologies to the teaching of violin to the very young. His original contributions are a truly great accomplishment and enrichment of the art of violin teaching.

CHAPTER 8

DR. SUZUKI AND ZEN: THE SPIRITUAL ELEMENT

Near the close of World War II as Dr. Suzuki looked at the starving children in the mountains of Kiso-Fukushima, he said, "Civilization is a mistake."[63] It is my belief that Dr. Suzuki's Talent Education movement sprang from this germinal statement. To articulate it further: Something is terribly askew with a world system that is unable to feed its children; we must find a new way of educating people that will produce better results.

Dr. Suzuki is famous for his pithy sayings and is oft-quoted in Suzuki studios around the globe somewhat in the tradition of "Confucius says." "Civilization is a mistake" is just such a saying. Typically, it is delicious in its understatement.

Dr. Suzuki's sayings always suggest an action to be taken, whether overtly or covertly. A whole series of actions on Dr. Suzuki's part, with reverberations felt around the world, have resulted from that single apprehension "Civilization is a mistake." It was perhaps a classic "ah-ha" experience.

Dr. Suzuki was already a music educator with a half-born system of violin pedagogy in his mind and heart when he articulated these words. He was forty-seven years old and had survived two grueling years at Kiso-Fukushima and was yet to undergo a period of physical illness that nearly claimed his life.

He survived both ordeals by harking back to the teachings of Dogen, a Zen priest he had studied as a youth. Dogen had taught him to live as best he could no matter what the circumstances and this he did at Kiso-Fukushima. Chinese medicine almost miraculously restored Dr. Suzuki to health after many Western approaches and remedies had been tried.

Dogen is a very famous Zen teacher, so again we see Dr. Suzuki being nurtured by the very best, highest, and finest available: Dogen, Einstein, Klingler. Klingler was a student of Joachim, thus putting Suzuki in touch with the oral tradition of the Franco-Belgian school of violin technique. Dr. Suzuki was indeed nurtured by love and has borne fruit accordingly with his Talent Education movement.

"Civilization is a mistake." This reaction of Dr. Suzuki to the devastation of World War II has had far-reaching results. Spiritual education and/or the re-making of entire civilizations is not easily accomplished. As with the re-education or rehabilitation of an individual it requires spiritual agency to succeed and is often best accomplished obliquely or by attacking some other more tangible goal which indirectly results in the necessary re-education or rehabilitation of spirit. But even before World War II, Suzuki as a youth of seventeen was deeply affected by children. He did enough school work to get by but was most fascinated with works that searched for the meaning of life. He diligently studied the sayings of the priest Dogen entitled *Shushogi*. He read Tolstoy and was fascinated by his "conscience." But his greatest joy was playing with the neighborhood children.[64]

From Mozart's music he learned that the life force itself is the whole basis for people's existence. The image of young, growing children took hold of his imagination at the same time. He saw them as the very essence of life's joy. This he describes as the origin of Talent Education.[65]

He loved children, spent time with them and realized how precious they were, and wanted to become as one of them, yet:

> Most of these beautiful children would eventually become adults filled with suspicion, treachery, dishonesty, injustice, hatred, misery, gloom. Why? Why couldn't they be brought up to maintain the beauty of their souls? There must be something wrong with education. That was when I first began to think along these lines.[66]

Calligraphy, archery, the martial arts had been used for centuries as disciplines to develop the spirit. Why shouldn't violin playing be the same sort of discipline? Begun at a very early age and taught perfectly to all, it could indeed contribute mightily to correcting the mistake that has been called civilization. It could produce beautiful, gentle human beings like those who played chamber music with Dr. Suzuki in Vienna: people like Dr. Michaelis, like Albert Einstein. People who were innovative thinkers, creative geniuses, cultured citizens of the world, gentle lovers of humanity.

These are the kinds of beautiful human beings the Talent Education movement seeks to create. It must begin with children, small children, for children learn what is in their environment. "Man is a Son of His Environment" as Dr. Suzuki puts it in one of his works of calligraphy. Whatever a child is immersed in, he or she will learn. A child from a dysfunctional home emerges a dysfunctional adult. A child from a beautiful healthy home emerges a beautiful, healthy adult. It cannot be otherwise. The story of two little girls brought up by a wolf documents this in an astonishing manner. Two little girls raised by a wolf were found northwest of Calcutta in a jungle zone.

The head, breast and shoulders of both children were covered with thick hair: they ran fast on all fours like a dog and people could not overtake them. Their shoulders were wide, their legs powerful with bent thighs that would not stretch out straight.[67]

Other physical adaptations are described. These were not inherited. They were adaptations made by the children's desire to survive, their life force.

Now, in our society we don't actually throw our children to the wolves. But the poor environment some have to experience after birth hurts and damages their developing abilities to such an extent that it is almost as bad as having been raised by wolves.[68]

Dr. John Bradshaw in his books, tapes and television series makes the same point. He doesn't say "some" children have a poor environment; he says that *all* families are to some extent dysfunctional because we are all coming out of the "mistake" that has been known by some as enlightenment— Bradshaw calls it "endarkenment."[69] Bradshaw has become a child advocate whose book *Homecoming* is an explanation of how to reclaim and champion your inner child. This process is ultimately spiritual as Bradshaw describes in "Wonder Child as Imago Dei," in Chapter 14 of the book.[70] Bradshaw also talks about the wounded child as the archetype of our century. Suzuki was one of the earliest articulators and responders to this archetype. His solution is also ultimately a spiritual solution: total education from infancy that always respects the spiritual life force in each and every child. People are children of their environment and whatever they are immersed in they will learn.

Dr. Suzuki has articulated many such unnoticed, intuitively obvious, precepts throughout the years as his Talent

Education movement has unfolded. The ability to do this is often the hallmark of a great innovator. Once the precept has been articulated, everyone wonders why they themselves hadn't thought to mention such an obviously correct idea. An example, "All Japanese children learn to speak Japanese."

Dr. Suzuki has shown the same talent with his use of various technologies, some of them very simple, to aid in the acquisition of the skill of violin playing. His use of cellophane tape to mark the placement of fingers is one such example. None of his technologies are incredibly arcane or complex. They are so simple as to be strokes of genius.

But what more exactly is the honoring of this spiritual life force in the children? This spiritual aspect of the Suzuki approach can be felt in the charisma it seems to exude. Many people can feel this readily but it is difficult to rationalize and discuss.

A particular difficulty can be seen in some learners' lip service to Dr. Suzuki's statement that the idea is not to develop professional violinists but to create beautiful human beings. They agree but also bend every effort and energy to technical mastery. Often there is an almost compulsive, fanatical obsession to do just exactly everything Dr. Suzuki might ever have said to do every day. If one truly attempts this, there would be little time for anything else. By the time records had been listened to, tapes played along with, repertoire played through, and new pieces worked on, little time would remain in the day for even an intermediate student to do anything else. Some teachers try to fit in all the old familiar etudes along with this, which really can present a challenge.

Observing Dr. Suzuki teach in his studio at the Institute in Matsumoto, I have been struck with the relaxed, friendly atmosphere. It is not the studio of a rigid, slave-driving master. Somehow, parents and teachers who get so wrapped up in the techniques and routines miss the essential spirit that really gives life to the Suzuki Method.

But what is this contradictory spirit that relaxes and lives in the moment, yet also churns out ten books of repertoire to be memorized (always ready to play), tapes, records, exercise books? What is it? How can there be so much emphasis on technical mastery and at the same time a seeming lack of concern?

The answer can be found in Zen. Remember, Dr. Suzuki was a student of Dogen as a youth. Zen is so pervasive a part of the Japanese way of life that the difficulties it might present to Westerners are probably incomprehensible, not even considered by Dr. Suzuki. Yet we practical Westerners really can't conceive of going through a process so difficult and painstaking as learning to play the violin, without having being able to *play* the thing as our major goal. Yet as Herrigel explains in *Zen in the Art of Archery,* immersion in Zen predisposes the Oriental mind to viewing the pursuit of very intricate skills—archery, ink painting, theater, tea ceremony, swordsmanship, dare I add playing the violin—as a spiritual exercise, a mystical exercise.[71]

Violin and bow are only a pretext for something that could happen just as well without them. They are a way to the goal of immediate experience. They are not the goal itself. They are aids to immediate apprehension of self and being. Expertise is not the goal at all. It is a means to the other goal, which everything is actually, as everyone knows who knows anything about Zen.

One of the great difficulties about Zen is that, according to experts, you either understand it or you don't. If you don't experience it, you can't understand it or have it explained to you. This is a very elementary concept in Zen. Nothing could be more ludicrous than someone explaining Zen to someone else. You either experience it or you don't.

It is with some hesitation, then, that I suggest that perhaps Zen permeates Dr. Suzuki's violin Method. It was with even greater apprehension that I rode the train from Tokyo to Matsumoto, trying to formulate some way of approaching the matter with Dr. Suzuki, yet not appearing totally inane. I had tried to find an express train from Tokyo to Matsumoto but with my lack of Japanese language skills I had ended up on the milk run stopping at every village en route. It took me ten hours to get to Matsumoto. That was perhaps just as it should have been considering what I was pondering.

It did occur to me as the train chugged through Tachikawa and I tried to get comfortable in seats that were too small for me that perhaps we Westerners weren't really so totally divorced from Zen. As I watched the Japanese businessmen and students settling into seats around me, I wondered if they all knew something secret about the world that escaped me or the Western mind.

Somehow, I think not. I'm not an expert on Zen but I've read a good deal on the subject and must confess to thinking I have had those moments of immersion in the immediate that make it possible to comprehend, if somewhat dimly, the goal that Zen enthusiasts are seeking. It seems to me not unlike that illusive commodity, mental health. If one could work through all one's Freudian, Jungian, and Adlerian hang-ups, one could live in a state of mental health that would be very much like living totally in the present or now, which seems to be something like Zen. There are spiritual disciplines in the West now that approximate this approach. The anonymous or twelve-step programs (based on the ancient Tao) now sweeping the United States also talk about annihilating the self or ego and living in the now.

The approach used by Zen is altogether less expensive, more pleasant and less nerve-wracking than our Western psychoanalysis and carries no stigma of being only for those who are insane or tottering on the brink of nervous breakdown. I don't know what comparative success rates might show, but I suspect it is as hard to become totally immersed in Zen as it is to be successfully psychoanalyzed or live totally immersed in the now on a continuing basis.

Another analogy between psychoanalysis and Zen is the need for the guidance of a skilled teacher and master. This is another reason Zen adepts tend not to pass along written instructions for progressing along the way. There must be personal instruction.

A most difficult concept is the annihilation of self. This seems quite different from perceptions of self-worth and OKness that are now popular with many psychological theories such as transactional analysis. There is an element of *sane* perception of self here which could perhaps be the annihilation Zen talks of. This is perhaps the same thing seen from different angles. I can easily affirm that I need to feel "OK" or not carry about a load of inferiority feelings that will cause me to become intractably anxious, hostile, obsessed with myself or immersed in a superiority mirage or puerile martyrdom. I find it much harder to warm up to the idea of annihilating myself. Annihilating the self is perhaps somewhat akin to dissolving obsession with self. Annihilating the ego or self could lead to achieving a healthy level of respect for that greater self in which we are all immersed. And it is immersion in the now and that greater self that is required for mastery violin playing and that is also its reward.

Watching Dr. Suzuki teach in his studio in Matsumoto seems to me very like the instructions in archery described by Herrigel in his *Zen in the Art of Archery.* Lessons with Dr. Suzuki seem similar, too. There is an unfailing kindness, yet a very definite insistence that he knows what he is doing and you are not doing what he wants you to do.

There are certain differences between the bowing technique used by many American and Western teachers and the bowing technique as Dr. Suzuki teaches it. The basic difference is Dr. Suzuki's concept of using the whole arm at all times, as opposed to Galamian's use of wrist, forearm, elbow at various precise and specified times.

I remember watching several other Western students being coached on this and then stepping up for my turn. I did not do better than anyone else, although I was quite sure I knew just what was wanted and felt quite discouraged. The other Westerners went to great lengths, explaining to me the exact technical differences and just what it was I had to do, to no avail. Dr. Suzuki listened quietly to all the chatter and patiently watched all my unsuccessful efforts. Finally, he showed me once more what he wanted; note that he *showed* me, he didn't discuss the theory of what he wanted. I tried again and failed. "You keep trying." he said, "I will tell you when you do it." That was the end of the lesson for that day.

The next time I visited Matsumoto was a year later in February of 1977. I did not bring my violin because I intended to work on this book and wanted to devote all of my energies to this end. Dr. Suzuki was not too pleased that I didn't have my violin with me and said there was something particular that he still wanted to teach me about my bowing technique.

One afternoon after lunch, the teacher trainees were having a group lesson with Dr. Suzuki in the small auditorium. I was observing the session scribbling away furiously in my notebook. Dr. Suzuki motioned me to join the group on stage and said he now would teach me the particular point he had in mind about my bowing.

I was to pretend I had my violin and play along with the group as they worked on the Vivaldi A Minor Concerto. I complied. Dr. Suzuki took particular pains to show me certain details about my bow grip and the movement of my bow arm. I adjusted my positions. He declared that I was executing the motions properly at the end of the session. I was elated.

One of the teacher trainees came up to me after the class and confessed, "I really didn't know what to make of you wandering around here scribbling notes all the time. Now I can see that you really are okay: you really do know how to play the violin." I thanked her and we had an amiable chat. Later that

111

evening I smiled as it occurred to me that she still really hadn't seen me play the violin at all. The whole session had been conducted with an imaginary violin. Or would Dr. Suzuki say a "spiritual" violin?

As in archery, so with violin playing: concentration may be one of the supreme goals. Dr. Suzuki, in particular, stresses concentration on the sound being produced. Technique must be so automatic as to be effortless, but the beauty of sound is something the player should always be very keenly aware of. There is a beauty of tone produced by Dr. Suzuki and his students, a quality of tone that is unique.

Here one aspect of the spiritual element abiding in this approach can be experienced. "Tone has living soul," says Dr. Suzuki. This is one of his calligraphy drawings reproduced and given to visitors. When all elements are correct, the tone will express through you and your violin. This is the special beautiful tone of the Suzuki violinist. Getting the elements correct is worked at through the many tonalization exercises throughout the curriculum. When it does express through you, you will know it and so will everyone else in the room. It is an electrifying experience.

Dr. Suzuki's insistence on, and many efforts to make less arduous (listening to records, playing with tapes, group lessons, group concerts), the learning of the technically masterable parts of violin playing to the point of repletion is also reminiscent of Zen. The outward execution of a piece must occur automatically, whether it is "Twinkle" or a Mozart violin concerto. One of Dr. Suzuki's most famous sayings among my students is "Once you have memorized the piece and it is perfectly correct and automatic, then you can begin to make music." This I heard him tell students in his Matsumoto studio many times. For a skill to become spiritual, to get to the point where you can "make music", a concentration of all the physical and psychic forces is needed. There is practice, repetition and repetition of the repeated.

Another Zen-like element in Dr. Suzuki's teaching is the way a piece is first introduced to the student. The student hears the piece before ever playing it. She hears and sees her teacher play the piece before she tries to learn it. She hears and sees other students play many of the advanced pieces long before she will actually tackle them herself.

Dr. Suzuki also makes use of the master teacher, a Zen way of teaching, by using the mother in starting very young pupils. This seems to be pure innovation on his part. He tells of recognizing how much a mother has to do with teaching a child its native tongue, and deciding to try and capitalize on this very fine teaching relationship. The mother learns violin first, then participates in teaching her child.

Dr. Suzuki recalls being in Germany to study with Klingler, post-World War I, and struggling mightily with the language. He remembers his chagrin when he would see two- and three-year-old children rushing about, babbling German as if it were the easiest thing in the world. He remembers his amazement at how they seemed to handle so easily what was so difficult for him. Perhaps this is when it first occurred to him that it might be possible to teach very small children very difficult things.

So the children repeat and repeat and slowly learn. They model after the mother who is also learning to play the violin. Then one day something happens. They may have been playing for two or three years. Suddenly, one of the songs, usually a simpler song, is played in an original, intuitive, creative manner. Instead of just copying and repeating and mimicking, the child is making music for the first time. It is a beautiful moment, often, perhaps, most beautiful for the teacher because the teacher may be the only one to recognize, at first what has happened. This is surely a peak experience, if not a Zen experience.

Another very exciting moment occurs earlier on when a child first realizes that he or she can actually manage and master the instrument. Every child can do this and it is very exciting when this realization sets in. Often parents and brothers and sisters may not really believe it is possible. Their distrust contaminates the student and it is a moment of great exhilaration, self-awareness and sharing when the child realizes that, with the help of the teacher, it can be done.

The relationship of the teacher and pupil is very important. There is an alertness to the pupil that is very much like the perceptive listening of Carl Rogers. The teacher perceives just what example, encouragement, practice, the student needs and gives it. Intense concentration is required for this; it is often almost palpable in Dr. Suzuki's studio.

A curious phenomenon is the lack of timidity displayed by Dr. Suzuki's students generally. Of course, they have played publicly since an early age, which might explain the phenomenon, but intense concentration on just what is being done or accomplished might be a better explanation. There are generally ten to fifteen people present in Dr. Suzuki's studio when he teaches and yet there is such intense concentration by the student who is working with Dr. Suzuki that there is a feeling of being lost in time or space. There is very little talking in the room, although the people assembled may be a talkative lot who know each other well. The racket of the *kenkyusei*'s room, where there generally seem to be at least twenty people, all playing the violin or talking at once, is in stark contrast. The silence could be simply because Dr. Suzuki is there, but I think more accurately it results from the intense concentration on what he is doing.

In the traditional Japanese arts, Zen teachers transfer the spirit of their art to their pupils. In a very real sense, I believe Dr. Suzuki does this, and teachers trained in his tradition do the same. Even at very elementary levels I have felt a definite need for concentration and some kind of transference when teaching beginners and, more especially, intermediate students. There is something that talking, demonstrating, playing, doesn't quite

114

do. A little psychic something more must happen. I believe the talk of immediate psychic communication is not just a figure of speech but a tangible reality. Occasionally, when I get tired of verbalizing fingerings I just "think" them to my students and they get them just as well. This can be startling to the parents who suddenly see their child playing a new passage seemingly without knowing the fingering. This is not a marvelous phenomenon of some kind. It is something anyone and everyone can do in the right atmosphere of communication and concentration of mind power.

Another influence of Zen on the Suzuki Method can be seen in the importance given to relaxation by Dr. Suzuki. Tension is one of the major obstacles to fine violin playing and Dr. Suzuki gives the problem constant attention as he works with the *kenkysei* (teacher trainees) in his studio. In his booklet for the annual teachers' meeting in the spring of 1976, Dr. Suzuki said, "We must teach the children the proper kind of relaxation. We can borrow the advice that Oriental teachers give to students of the martial arts of sword and karate. From early times, martial arts teachers have explained how to be relaxed and yet centered, ready for instantaneous action." William Starr in his *The Suzuki Violinist* tells of *Ki* (coordination of mind and body) and how its practitioners can help violinists. Specific, practical suggestions are given for helping to keep violinists' arms and shoulders relaxed. "Combat upward tensions by keeping weight underside: think of the underside of your feet; holding the violin in position, think of the underside of both elbows. Now, play the violin, concentrating on playing the music. If your mind wanders, your posture will suffer."[72] Mr. Yoshihiki Hirata, a *Ki* instructor who, as a child, was a violin student in Dr. Suzuki's Talent Education program in Japan, has given a number of demonstrations in America on the application of *Ki* to violin instruction.[73]

If Dr. Suzuki's teaching is, indeed, permeated by Zen, just what does this mean? It means that the fantastic virtuosity that Dr. Suzuki can develop at a very early age in his students is not the main point of the whole exercise. It means that this virtuosity which so attracts and impresses Westerners is not the quintessential thing. It means Dr. Suzuki's use of the pedagogical techniques analyzed in this book and the phenomenal success he has achieved using them is again not the main thing. Even the demonstration that every human being has the potential for incredible virtuosity and mastery is not the main thing, important though it may be in this time of disregard for the value of the individual. The main thing is the self-knowledge that this experience in virtuosity brings about.

To make all this a little more concrete, let me pass on to you the explanation given to me by Toba Sensei over a lunch at a tempura house in Matsumoto. As explained earlier, Toba Sensei was one of Dr. Suzuki's outstanding students who toured in the United States for him in the 1950s. She had mastered the Suzuki repertoire and more. At the time of our discussion she had seventy students in Matsumoto, three of whom, at the age of eleven or twelve, were beyond the ten Suzuki books and into very difficult concert repertoire. "What has it done for you?," I asked her; "what has it done for your life to have achieved this mastery of the violin and of the art of teaching?" This was her answer:

> It taught me patience. That I could not achieve difficult things immediately, but if I continued to work and try, I would eventually be able to do things that had seemed impossible before. Anger, frustration, despair, giving up, accomplished nothing. Patience and hard work could accomplish a great deal. The accomplishment gave me confidence. If I could do this, I could do other things that seemed very difficult. I might not always be able to understand just exactly how, but if I didn't give up and

kept trying I could perhaps eventually solve any problem that I felt needed solving. The trying involves concentration. Success does not come about by magic but by full concentration of the mind and body on the problem. When solution to the problem comes, it may not be fully understood intellectually or rationally, but it is a solution because it works.

Not a bad collection of things for young people to learn about life, I thought. It sounds suspiciously like virtue, the thing that moralists and ministers prate on and on about, but which nonetheless seems conspicuously absent in public and private life. Perhaps it is more teachable through the concrete experience of mastering a difficult instrument than through sermons and memorization of rules and regulations. Perhaps it is more personal and more real when attained through one's own struggle with oneself in acquiring a difficult discipline.

It sounds suspiciously, too, like mental health. An antidote to suicide, murder, depression, divorce, dissension. If one becomes solidly grounded by discovering one's own value, worth, and human dignity through a struggle with a difficult discipline, mastered in one's own unique way, other life challenges can be faced and mastered as well. With the help of a sensitive and understanding teacher, who has found self-worth in the same way and will not intrude but will guide with respect and concern along the twisting path that leads to mastery, one can deal creatively with whatever life throws across one's path and overcome and succeed.

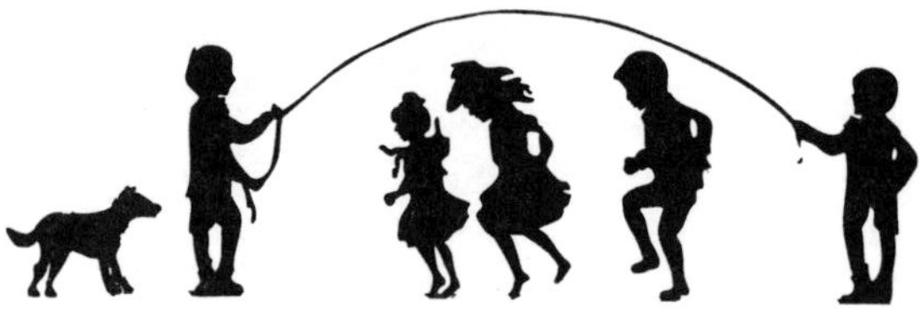

CHAPTER 9

REPLICATING THE SUZUKI MAGIC IN OTHER DISCIPLINES

Dr. Suzuki has reiterated many times that the success his students demonstrate is just a small taste of the success his method of teaching could create in any area. This was a matter of interest and concern at the June 1994 Convention of the Suzuki Association of the Americas in Chicago, Illinois. The theme of the Convention was "Creating a Learning Community." In his keynote address, "The Place of Children in the World Community," Dr. James Gabarino, president of the Erickson Institute for Advanced Study in Child Development, discussed the concern of his profession with children at risk. He shared findings that social toxicity is a daily experience for many of our children and that stressors put them at risk. More than one stressor causes the risk to accumulate. Stressors, as described by Dr. Gabarino, include drug-abusing parents; being exposed to rigid and punitive lifestyles; being a member of a minority group; living in a dangerous neighborhood. These stressors can accumulate to the point of lowering I.Q. Risk accumulates, but opportunity ameliorates. The antidote to this toxicity then is opportunity; opportunity can lower the impact of such stressors. In particular, the type of opportunity that ameliorates is opportunity to participate in activities that give meaning to children's lives, and in activities that involve some spiritual discipline. Involvement in a Suzuki Learning program provides both of the elements of Dr. Gabarino's antidote.[74]

Dr. Gabarino's address was both sobering and inspiring. It delineated the difficult situation of many children in our world today. This reality may not have been pleasant for the Suzuki assembly with its orientation toward positive thinking to contemplate; however, it is important not to confuse positive thinking with denial of reality. Facing unpleasant facts is necessary. The forces of positive thinking can then be used to deal constructively with any difficult challenge.

The inspiring part of Dr. Gabarino's message resided more in the heart of the assembled teachers than in his words. Any Suzuki teacher worth her salt would have known intuitively that the Suzuki Method offers many ways to present the type of opportunity that ameliorates to the children of the world. This is a very exciting realization and it is exactly what Dr. Suzuki envisioned when he embarked on the adventure of creating the method in the late forties.

Dr. Gabarino's challenge is most directly addressed by developments in the early childhood education (ECE) section of the Suzuki movement. While current programs are not now specifically aimed at children identifiably at risk (there may be many children whose potential is at risk who are not obviously imperiled) Suzuki ECE educators are creating ways of handling challenges and dilemmas that could be used in emergency situations as well as with the more routine contemporary difficulties that they are confronting.

Suzuki teachers in the Americas, for example, struggle with an apparent discrepancy between the Japanese and American approaches. Japanese children seem to be able to start at the age of two-and-one-half or three, as suggested by Dr. Suzuki, and proceed successfully with learning an instrument. This doesn't seem to happen as readily in the

Americas. Experienced teachers are commenting that whereas in their earlier teaching days they successfully started with two- and one-half and three-year-olds, that doesn't seem to be working today. Educator Dorothy Jones has seen this as a difference in the level of attention and education young children are receiving from their parents in the 1980s and 1990s. Latchkey kids are just not receiving the time and attention their parents formerly did. No one is singing to them; no one is reading to them; no one is talking to them. Jones works with this situation at her Children's Talent and Education Center in Ontario, Canada by enrolling students in baby/parent classes for ages zero to two and pre-instrumental classes from age two and up, with the children moving into instrumental study when they are socially and educationally ready to begin actual study of an instrument.[75] These classes have been so successful that Jones has gone on to continue with early childhood education, preschool and kindergarten classes and is now launching into the world of elementary education.

Susan Grilli also has recognized the potential of the Suzuki approach for early childhood education. She uses it to nurture parents as partners in the education of their children and, indeed, to nurture parents as teachers, for they are the first and most successful teachers of their children.

We have had woeful reports of late on how unsuccessful the American schools are at creating literacy and basic math and science skills in their students; but take note that none of the children in question are unable to speak their native tongue. Suzuki says *every* child can be educated to a very high level, and this is evidenced by their ability to speak their mother tongue. Suzuki has patterned his teaching method on how parents teach a child to speak its native language. This is a method of education that works. Many of our current approaches to later education apparently do not. The difference starts with Suzuki's basic premise that *every* child can be educated to a *very high* level. Notice that he does not say exactly the same level but to a very high level; learning to speak a language is a very high level of achievement.

Thus, energy and excitement is being generated about the great benefits of transferring the Suzuki educational technology to other disciplines. Perhaps the level of success achieved with music of instruments can be replicated in mathematics, science, and language arts. Strangely enough, actual transferences at the moment are occurring at the extremes of the educational spectrum. Grilli and Jones are working on the transfer at the level of early childhood education; I am using the technology at the university level, as is Paula Resch. Many other applications are sure to follow. Let us then take a closer, more detailed, look at the work of Grilli and Jones and at the model I am using. Then I would like to make some suggestions for further applications.

Grilli and Jones have successfully transferred Suzuki teaching technology to the field of early childhood education: Jones runs a school in London, Ontario, Canada and Grilli in New York City. Grilli first learned of the Suzuki Method in 1967 when she went to interview for a position at the public elementary school in Harwich, Massachusetts. There Sylvia Edward was using a Title III grant for experiments in creative education. She and Grilli developed a whole new curriculum tailoring the Suzuki approach to the needs of the children of Harwich in their public school setting.

One day a kindergartner said to Grilli, "I hate school but I love the violin." Investigating the genesis of this response, Grilli overheard a demeaning, domineering teacher cow a little student into submission, creating hatred of school and a sense of inferiority in the student in less than thirty-five words. Grilli was incensed and at the same time inspired to bring the Suzuki method, that had led the child to love the violin, to the whole curriculum.

Grilli observed Dr. Suzuki's experimental kindergarten in Matsumoto, Nagano Prefecture, Japan, and again felt inspired to incorporate the innovations she was seeing with a regular kindergarten curriculum. She was given a chance to do this at the Nischimachi International School in 1971. She found during a year of experimental teaching that Suzuki's ideas translated easily into projects in science, art, language, and math. As is true in the learning of musical instruments, when the children were led by a teacher who assumed they had unlimited potential, the learning was rapid and beyond general levels of expectation.

Upon returning to the United States, Grilli joined the faculty of the School for Strings, a Suzuki string school in New York City. There she felt drawn to the potential of creating a Suzuki early-childhood education situation for children at the same age as the two-and-one-half-year-old beginning Suzuki violin students. In October 1974 she and two other teachers began The Suzuki Pre-School.

The School has gone through several moves, searching to incorporate a rich learning environment as part of its setting. It is now a part of the Hastings Talent Education Center in Manhattan. Here, preschoolers can move smoothly into advanced programs as they graduate.

Grilli is not merely adding Suzuki violin to a preschool learning situation. The school approaches each subject area in the Suzuki style. The school has been approved by Dr. Suzuki and offers teacher training workshops approved by the Suzuki Association of the Americas.

Grilli stresses that the Suzuki idea has far greater educational implications than its musical application. These implications include philosophy and method but, most importantly, emanate from the spirit of Suzuki teaching: "the inspiration to reach beyond oneself into the innermost recesses of creativity and imagination residing in each of us"[76] and teach and learn from that place of love and innovation.

Another important application of the Suzuki approach is involving parents in children's learning. Parents are still the most successful educators known, as they successfully teach their children to speak a language—an achievement that is at a very high level of learning. Many other educators fail miserably when compared to this level of accomplishment. Including these successful parent educators as part of the teaching/learning team and doing it effectively is one of the great coups of the Suzuki approach. The method the parents use to teach children their native tongue is also used in the approach. Sequential learning reinforced with love and delight is the heart of the Mother-Tongue approach which is another name Suzuki gives his method. The learning team is seen as a triangle with child as learner, parent as coach, and teacher as guide. Working this triangle is a fine art that Suzuki teachers learn through practice and training. This can be replicated in any discipline. An essential part of the triangle is the honoring and respecting of all other points of the triangle.

In Chapter One of her book, *Preschool in the Suzuki Spirit*, Grilli describes in detail another important aspect of the triangle—the parent and teacher bringing the richness of their experience and cultural traditions into the learning triangle. As the contributions and creativity of all are honored, a very rich learning environment is created.

In a 1993 booklet entitled *Nurturing Parents as Teachers*, Susan Grilli elaborates on the Suzuki process of incorporating parents as partners in the learning process. Grilli comments that "this approach is a natural because it reaffirms for parents what they already know better than anyone, that children meet the expectations we have of them."[77]

> Based on the unselfconscious and delightful way parents teach their native language to their children, Suzuki early educators hope to unlock the natural inventiveness in any adult who is teaching a very young child. The immediate goal is the parent as a rich learning resource for the child, and the reward is the parent and child

learning together with pleasure and without introducing the concept of competition. The Suzuki approach has been used to teach many instruments, singing, preschool, kindergarten, and now is inspiring more and more progress in early childhood education.[78]

In *Nurturing Parents as Teachers,* Grilli goes on to detail preschool projects in five learning areas: language, art, music, math, and science. Her presentation is particularly good on introducing math and science so that children will find them exciting and fun and not develop anxiety and neuroses about their ability to perform in these areas. Grilli also stresses the importance of making connections between these five areas and suggests projects integrating these areas as they so often are found connected in everyday life.

Adapting the Suzuki approach to preschool teaching is the core of Grilli's book, *Preschool in the Suzuki Spirit.* Detailed instructions for those interested can be found in perusing the book.

Another very important gift the Suzuki approach can give is that of enhancing the self-esteem of its students. Positive feedback is programmed into each lesson. The value of this self esteem cannot be overrated. Low self-esteem is at the base of many types of behavioral disorders among children and adults and this facet of the Suzuki approach alone could contribute to alleviating the skyrocketing incidence of all types of addiction and emotional illness in our society.

John Bradshaw details very minutely in the first part of his book, *Creating Love,* what happens to children when they are subjected to the stressors mentioned by Dr. James Gabarino in his keynote address at the 1994 Suzuki Association of the Americas Convention. Those stressors included living with addict caretakers and persons who are emotionally ill. In the second part of his book, Bradshaw talks about ways to ameliorate effects of a childhood spent in this type of environment. Just as involvement in a Suzuki program was seen as a way to ameliorate risks to children while they are in a difficult environment—risks accumulate and negatively affect I.Q.; whereas opportunity ameliorates—using Suzuki techniques can also aid adults who were negatively impacted by being raised in a dysfunctional environment.

Bradshaw describes the healing process required as "demystification" and lists many healing processes. Among these processes are reprogramming and remapping the self. Suzuki-style work with audio tapes for positive self-programming could fit very comfortably into his lexicon of curative modalities. This, then, is another possible application of the Suzuki experience. According to Bradshaw, "Our patriarchal, nationalist child-rearing and educational practices have tried to lead us away from childhood. We need the foundation that childhood supplies. We need to hold on to the wisdom and talents of childhood. We need a pedagogy and education that elicits and expands our childhood ways of knowing."[79] The Suzuki Method *is* that pedagogy and that education.

The Suzuki Method not only provides this pedagogy and education but challenges the violence that is often the means of "educating" in other modalities. Bradshaw states that violence always wounds the child. The great potential of each child, its capacity for "soulfulness," as Bradshaw calls it, would emerge spontaneously if the child could develop without violence. There are other means of informing and educating. Suzuki says very directly that there is to be no punishing in his method of education. He intuitively prohibits negative conditioning, which Western psychologists have demonstrated to be an ineffective means of education. Yet physical violence is still practiced in families, and many other forms of negative conditioning are practiced in our schools and society. Negative conditioning doesn't work. It wounds rather than educating. What is learned from violent punishment (I am not OK) harms the child rather than preparing him or her to deal effectively with life. Application of this insight alone would free our children of the wounding that stifles and mutilates them. It would open the path for the wisdom and talent of childhood to be elicited and expanded by enlightened parenting, pedagogy, and education.

Whatever the application of the Suzuki Method, learning to use it well requires individual creativity in applying successful Suzuki principles to any particular discipline. Assuming the individual desirous of using Suzuki principles is already well-rehearsed and trained in a subject area, responsible experimentation with use of Suzuki ideas could follow.

Learning to use the Suzuki approach as a teacher is very much an individual process. Once a teacher is familiar with the Suzuki principles, it is then that teacher's own creative process and adventure to apply them to the particular disciplines and learning situation with which he or she is involved. Grilli details how she has done this in *Preschool in the Suzuki Spirit*. A similar process would have to ensue for others in different disciplines, to use the Suzuki approach. This is one of the great strengths of the approach: it can be adapted to different disciplines and situations. It is flexible and adaptable; it is not a rigid set of mechanical rules that must be applied in a certain way.

Paula Resch talks about using the Suzuki approach in elementary and secondary school writing programs in her "Suzuki and the Teaching of Writing: A Surprising Connection."[80] Resch, a college English professor, describes a connection between process writing, or the writing renaissance, as some call it, and the Suzuki approach.

What I want to show is that these two methods have a lot in common and teachers of writing should recognize that if they use the process method they are not working in an educational vacuum, but, like Suzuki teachers, are making important strides in humanizing young people in a technological age.[81]

Resch describes the least concrete but perhaps the most important connection between the two movements as being the idea that every child can be a musician or writer. "All children can write and make music."[82] All children can be educated to a very high level, as Suzuki has often said, and that holds for all discipline areas.

Another similarity Resch noticed is that, just as in process writing, children are encouraged to write whole stories, poems and articles; Suzuki students are given "real" music and begin with entire folk songs—not bits and pieces. The study of bits and pieces—grammar in writing, etudes in music—is not nearly as central as in traditional approaches. In addition, students are told that they can write or make music very well. Mastery learning is encouraged from the beginning. The Suzuki student keeps his or her musical repertoire for life—ever fine-tuning and making each piece a more beautiful musical expression.

> The new writing teachers encourage multiple drafts of the writing project so that the student can enter more into the writing process as professionals . . . We . . . encourage students to do the kind of fine tuning that engages them in the process of adding, deleting, substituting and rearranging that are central to authentic writing.[83]

Another similarity noted by Resch is group work. A process writing classroom has an ambiance similar to a Suzuki group lesson. Rather than working on a difficult skill in isolation, students work with teacher, parents, or peers in small and large groups and one-on-one sessions. They hone and improve their skills through creating performances or pieces of writing in a learning community.

Resch observes that the teacher's role is also similar in the two styles of teaching while differing from other approaches. The Suzuki teacher is a model but also a fellow participant. In concerts, at group lessons, even individual lessons, Suzuki students often make music with their teacher. They are often involved together in the process of making music. Similarly, Resch, as a college teacher, opens herself to participating in the projects she suggests for her students. She throws herself into the in-class writing process as teacher participant and lets her students see her search for the right word and experiment with possibilities. Thus, in her teaching of writing, Resch has adapted approaches from the Suzuki method that her own children experience at their Suzuki music lessons.

This is also one of the techniques I have appropriated in using the Suzuki Method to teach English composition at the college level. I teach advanced English Composition for George Mason University in Fairfax, Virginia. The course is catalogued as Engl 302 and students are required to take the course in their third year of university work. The idea is that at this point their writing can be based in their chosen area of specialization for some of their assignments. I have chosen to teach this course for the past seven years and have taught seven to eight sections of that course per academic year during this time. This has enabled me to focus on using the Suzuki methodology while holding variables to a minimum.

The first Suzuki concept that I use is that of positive reinforcement. In the first class I tell my students that I believe each of them has great potential as a writer and that during the class I will be seeking ways to bring out that potential and make it real, in the form of excellent pieces of writing. I believe that each one of them has the potential to be a successful writer. This is rather startling to some students who have been beaten down by our system of grading and unloving teaching.

Nevertheless, I reiterate that I believe and know from experience that everyone can be a successful writer and can write at a very high level if they go through the process of revising, correcting, and deleting that all professional writers practice. I also tell them that everyone who goes through the necessary process and produces that excellent piece of writing will get an A. I will explain to the dean if everyone in the class has an A. They seem delighted with this idea and, as a result a positive attitudes and an atmosphere of total success as a very real possibility are being created. This is a necessary first step in creating a learning community based on positive reinforcement.

Next, I work with the class as a group to create a kind of forum of listeners in which we give feedback as to effectiveness of communication, but we do not get into argumentation or discussion of content. I request that, when students give feedback to one another in the large group or even small group sessions, they always preface any suggestions for improvement with positive feedback on what was good and effective about a paper. This is, of course, straight out of Suzuki's suggestions on how to teach. I emphasize that everyone in the class, including myself, is entitled to his or her opinion and we are not going to try and change anyone's opinion about anything—we are just going to work on how effectively we communicate our opinion or information, whatever it may be.

This creates a safe atmosphere in which to share honestly. The safety is very important in music as in the composition situation. In order to express creatively, one has to be able to risk articulating and expressing who one really is in the playing of an instrument or in writing.

The first assignment I give is an intellectual autobiography; this helps to create the forum of supportive listeners. Each person is, of course, an expert on his or her autobiography, so the class gets practice in focusing only on the effectiveness of communication and not criticizing content.

Writers learn to receive feedback on whether or not they communicated what they intended. This is very similar to the kind of learning that goes on in Suzuki's group lessons when the students discuss with the teacher and one another the effectiveness of a performance after one student has done a solo during the group lesson.

As the students share their autobiographies, they get to know one another and a creative supportive feeling evolves because no one is criticized or put down; intense effort is made at helping each other to improve. A learning community is being created. This is the equivalent of the atmosphere created at regular Suzuki group lessons that students attend month after month. A kind of community of acceptance and enhancement of positive growth is created. All are supported in reaching for their highest potential while each individual is accepted as is, as well.

Individual tuition or private music lessons are approximated during individual writing conferences. Just as a music student cannot progress well on an instrument without individual tutoring, writers also need this kind of attention. I have an individual conference with each student on each paper. I grade the paper during the individual conference. The conferences are preceded by large group sessions during which students read their paper to the entire class and get very spirited input and feedback from their peers. A particular advantage of these sessions is that the writers get information on whether they have actually communicated what they intended to communicate. I encourage each writer to ask very direct questions of peers regarding the effect desired and if this actually was achieved. By the time students get to me for individual conferences they have also had several small group sessions on their papers. These sessions occur before and during the individual conferences and are the students' final input before grading.

Grading is a challenge and can be demoralizing to students. I often wish I didn't have to grade students, because it interferes with the process of educating them. At our present level of advancement, it seems to be unfortunately unavoidable. I handle this as positively as possible for myself and the students by seeing the grade as a function of the time and effort put into a project rather than a measure of a student's inherent worth or potential. I encourage them to revise, revise, revise; I suggest they get input and feedback from many sources—large group, small group, roommates, parents, whomever—before they appear with their finished product for grading. Their grade is created by the time and energy they have available to expend on this process. Dr. Suzuki often says "go home and practice this 10,000 times." Anyone can learn anything with the right guidance and the requisite number of repetitions. How well students do is a result of their starting point and how much time they had to revise and rework. This sort of approach ameliorates the discouraging effect that required grading can have on students, and keeps it from interfering with the positive atmosphere required to truly educate by nurturing, encouraging, and informing.

I have tried to match the motivational aspects in the Suzuki Studio of concerts, recitals, and performances with the publication of students' works insofar as this is possible. I collate collections of the students' essays and reproduce them as examples of what I want for future classes. I let the students choose to whom they would like to send their essays and have sent collected essays on world peace to Gorbachov, President Bush, the Pope, the Secretary General of the United Nations. I have letters of commendation on file from many of the above! Collected essays on ameliorating the damage of gender stereotyping have been sent to the Secretary of Health, Education, and Welfare. Most recently a collection of essays on positive ways of dealing with the AIDS epidemic included poems and short stories from students, as well as the required expository essays. The collection was well received among Fairfax County health authorities, officials at the American Federation of Teachers, and in the English Department at George Mason University. This is a testimony to the quality of writing being produced as a result of using the Suzuki Method to teach English composition, but more importantly it motivates and inspires other students to achieve and create at a similarly high level. Students feel honored when I ask them if I can include their essays in one of the next collections and they often revise and provide clean copy even *after* they have been graded. This is very real testimony to their integrity and valuing of excellence for its own sake. Here I see the Suzuki Method succeeding in creating those fine human beings who are Dr. Suzuki's ultimate goal in the Suzuki educational process.

Sharing my struggle with work on this book has been a major way I have worked as teacher participant in the Suzuki style with my students at George Mason. They love the story of how a reading of the first page of the "finished" manuscript (at ten years into the process) by a friend produced input on an obvious grammar glitch that no one—not myself, not typists, not proofreaders—had caught. They rejoiced with me as four contracts to publish the book rolled in after I mailed out forty-five copies of the manuscript to possible publishers selected from *Writer's Market* during the winter blizzards of early 1994, this after being blocked for three years after the first rejection of my manuscript. We have been amazed when what I have often described to my students as my ideal of a really fine experience for them in creating their research papers actually happened to me as I did the work for the final chapter of this book. Investigating something you really care about and passing on your findings via your writing and documentation is that ideal for me; this has happened as I write and as I coincidentally stumbled over the listing of Paula Resch's article in a bibliography mentioned only in passing in a presentation on research at the 1994 Suzuki Association of the Americas

Convention.[84] My excitement over the research findings was shared by librarians at George Mason and my students as we pulled Resch's opinion paper from its ERIC microfiche, reproduced it and saw how "right on" it was for the purpose of this chapter.

A final joke on me, which my students totally appreciated and which is more than a little suggestive of that mysterious Zen element that floats in and out of the entire Suzuki approach, was my apprehension that my work on this last chapter was going to have to be more creative than research-based. I like to assign solution papers in keeping with the positive basis of the Suzuki approach. I like to hear solutions, not problems. Favorite topics are solving international conflicts without using warfare, how to eliminate the negative effects of gender stereotyping, solutions for ecological issues, and more. It is most often true that the solutions have to be created. There are reams of material on the problem but very little data is to be found on the solution. "You are not going to be able to do much research on this" is one of my favorite lines. I realized this was literally coming true for me in regard to the writing of this last chapter. My students enjoyed my dilemma, but as they have often expressed to me (after some initial grumbling), I have found it ultimately very exhilarating to be working on positive, creative solutions; it is being on the cutting edge of what is really important as we move into the twenty-first century.

So these are the de facto ongoing applications of the Suzuki Method to other disciplines: to early childhood education, to preschool and elementary school education, and to the teaching of English composition at the college and university level. Other possible applications are legion; there are no limits, so long as we use our creativity and flexibility.

Elizabeth Jones Cherwick has done a bibliography entitled "Preliminary Bibliography of Psychological and Educational Research Involving or Mentioning the Suzuki

Method." Her bibliography suggests that not only can the Suzuki "magic" be replicated in other disciplines, but that the method is a rich field for studies by educational psychologists and for educational research in general.[85] In addition Cherwick lists many other applications of the method: art and education for young children, developmental psychology, philosophy, learning to learn, language, mathematics, Spanish, psychology, psychoanalysis, education, aesthetics, early childhood education training of learning skills and attitudes, child development, writing, Piaget, cognition, prenatal learning, psychology of music, accelerated learning and teaching, cultural continuity, third world studies, and secondary education. This rather exhaustive list in a "preliminary" bibliography of psychological and educational areas is prophetic of the many possibilities for replicating the outstanding accomplishments of the Suzuki approach in other disciplines.

I have personally used the Suzuki approach in many different areas to facilitate learning. I have used it to erase old negative images from my past and program new positive attitudes into my memory bank. To do this, I taped the new positive messages to myself on audio cassettes and played them as often as possible and convenient, even when I was sleeping. This is the way Suzuki students listen to audio tapes of the music they are learning. It is an excellent way to build self-esteem and create new positive attitudes, and it is far less costly then psychotherapy (another way to do the same thing). It can also greatly enhance therapeutic work.

One of the most dramatic successes I have had personally in using the Suzuki approach in another discipline has been in language learning. My doctoral studies led me to choose a dissertation topic based partially on texts in Spanish by Jose Rizal. My dissertation committee decided that I would have to pass an exam in Spanish to use the Rizal material. I had two-and-one-half years in which to become proficient enough to pass the exam. This was a very short time for such a task.

After some angst, I decided to use the Suzuki approach and attempt it. I hired a tutor and taped every session. I listened to these tapes as I commuted back and forth to the University of the Philippines and played them while I was sleeping. These are tried and tested Suzuki learning techniques that work, but more important was my *knowing* that this approach worked and that learning occurred very efficiently with these approaches. In other words, I believed in and had validated faith that a positive approach using the Suzuki technique would be successful. It was. I passed the Spanish exam with no problem. I also successfully used audio tapes in the Suzuki way to prepare for my comprehensive exams for the doctorate. I passed all four of them easily on the first try, another testimony to the success of the Suzuki Method in fields other than music.

Actual applications and the knowledge generated by study of the success of the Suzuki approach will greatly enrich the many subject areas mentioned by Cherwick as well as our overall understanding of the educational process required to produce fine human beings. It is my fervent hope that this knowledge will be used to remedy the tragedy and loss in human terms that has resulted from the use of incorrect and barbarous methods of child-rearing. These mistaken methods have resulted in twisted personalities and great loss to humankind of the inherent potential greatness in all our children. Indeed, as I observe the results already achieved, I feel certain that the Suzuki approach is part of a whole new wave of creative educational and child-rearing techniques that will usher in a renaissance of realized human potential and a golden age of positive self-realization. This new age will see ever greater and greater numbers of individuals achieving the highest and best that is possible, both within and for themselves and without, and for individuals touched by their lives. This is the potential of the successful application of the Suzuki approach to all areas of learning. Let us hope that this potential will be realized rapidly for the happiness of all children and the positive evolution of the world for all people everywhere.

THE END

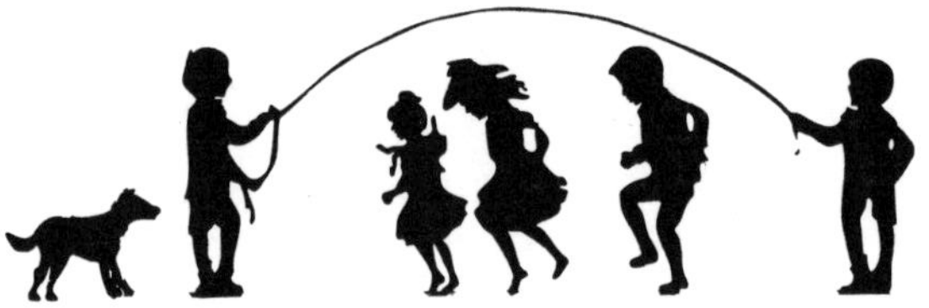

GLOSSARY OF TERMS

Classical Conditioning
The repeated pairing of two stimuli so that eventually a previously neutral stimulus (e.g., a bell ringing) comes to elicit the same response (salivation) as was previously elicited by the other stimulus (red meat). This was the type of conditioning first described by Pavlov, hence it is sometimes called Pavlovian conditioning.

Conditioning
A type of learning that is described in terms of changing relationships between stimuli, between responses, or between both stimuli and responses.

Mastery Learning
Learning to the point of almost total perfection. The Suzuki student learns a piece until he or she can't get it "wrong". This involves far more repetitions than the more traditional approach of studying something until you can get it right and then moving on. This perfection is commensurate with age and learning level. More advanced techniques are applied to earlier pieces as the student masters each new skill. This is another facet of mastery learning.

Modeling Behavior
Imitative behavior which involves the learning of a new response through seeing it modeled by someone else.

Operant Conditioning
A type of learning that involves an increase in the probability of a spontaneously emitted behavior re-occurring as a function of reinforcement. Most of the experimental work of B. F. Skinner

investigates the principles of operant conditioning, hence it is sometimes called Skinnerian conditioning.

Pedagogy
(pedagogical, *adj.*) The art or science of teaching.

Programmed Instruction
An auto-instructional procedure that makes use of the systematic presentation of information in small steps (frames), usually in the form of a textbook or employing some other device. Computers are often used to provide programmed instruction. Programs typically require the learner to make responses and provide him or her with immediate knowledge of results. The Suzuki curricula have many of the attributes of programmed instructional material, particularly if they are taught in the proper Suzuki manner.

Shaping Behavior
A technique whereby people are taught to perform complex behaviors that were not previously in their repertoire of behaviors. The technique involves reinforcing responses that become increasingly closer approximations to the desired behavior. Also called the method of successive approximations. This is almost exactly the kind of learning that is necessary to become adept at playing a musical instrument. The best teachers are very skilled at "shaping."

Student-centered Teaching
The term is derived from Carl Rogers' psychological concept of client-centered therapy. Rogers developed the idea of a type of patient-counselor relationship where the counselor was not directive in the sense of telling clients how they should behave, but rather attempted to allow the patients to express themselves and to discover within some ways of dealing with their own behavior. Student-centered teaching focuses on the student in

an analogous way. The student is valued as an equal in the learning process and input from the student is solicited and used. The learning process is thus individualized, or tailored, to each student.

Total Use of Technology

Related to programmed instruction, this is the use of whatever methodologies or machine technologies are available to aid instruction. This began with Sidney Pressey's teaching machines in 1932; there are now many forms of technology in wide use, including computer-aided instruction. The Suzuki approach uses many types of technology, including varying the size of instruments for beginners, audio cassettes, video cassettes, compact discs, and instant VCR playback during lessons.

NOTES

1. Shinichi Suzuki, *Nurtured by Love*, 2nd ed. (Secaucus, New Jersey: Summy-Birchard, 1983)59.

2. Suzuki, *Love*, 69.

3. Suzuki, *Love*, 71.

4. Suzuki, *Love*, 51.

5. Suzuki, *Love*, 72.

6. Suzuki, *Love*, 107-108.

7. Suzuki, *Love*, 73.

8. Suzuki, *Love*, 73.

9. Suzuki, *Love*, 74.

10. Suzuki, *Love*, 75.

11. Suzuki, *Love*, 78.

12. Suzuki, *Love*, 77.

13. Suzuki, *Love*, 77.

14. Suzuki, *Love*, 77.

15. Suzuki, *Love*, 78.

16. Suzuki, *Love*, 79.

17. Suzuki, *Love*, 78.

18. Suzuki, *Love*, 79.

19. Suzuki, *Love*, 79.

20. Suzuki, *Love*, 23.

21. Suzuki, *Love*, 20.

22. Suzuki, *Love*, 29.

23. Shinichi Suzuki, *Law of Ability and the "Mother Tongue" Method of Education*, Pamphlet for the Japan Institute of Educational Psychology (Matsumoto, Japan: Talent Education Institute, 1973) 11.

24. Shinichi Suzuki, *Bulletin for the Second International Conference on Talent Education* (Matsumoto, Japan: Talent Education Institute, 1977) 1.

25. Suzuki, *Love*, 40.

26. Suzuki, *Love*, 47.

27. Suzuki, *Love*, 101.

28. Clifford Cook, *Suzuki Education in Action* (Jericho, N.Y.: Exposition Press, 1970) 18-19.

29. Suzuki, *Love,* 103.

30. Suzuki, *Love,* 102.

31. "Fiddling Legions," *Newsweek* 25 March 1964: 73.

32. Suzuki, *Ability,* 3.

33. Suzuki, *Ability,* 3-4.

34. Suzuki, *Ability,* 4.

35. Suzuki, *Ability,* 19.

36. Suzuki, *Ability,* 18-19.

37. I.P. Pavlov, *Conditioned Reflexes* (London: Oxford University Press, 1927).

38. E.L. Thorndike, *Selected Writings from a Connectionist's Psychology* (New York: Appleton-Century-Crafts. 1949).

39. J.B. Watson, *Behaviorism* (Chicago: The University of Chicago Press, 1930).

40. Thorndike, *Selected Writings.*

41. B.F. Skinner, *Science and Human Behavior* (New York, Macmillan, 1953).

42. This is a fact I noted as a high school chemistry student memorizing information for an examination.

43. Michiru Hotaka. Letter to the author. 11 October 1991.

44. James Dobson, *Dare to Discipline* (Wheaton, Illinois: Tyndale House Publishers, 1979) 64.

45. Dobson 64.

46. B.F. Skinner, *Verbal Behavior* (New York: Appleton-Century-Crafts 1957).

47. Skinner, *Verbal Behavior.*

48. Guy R. LeFrancois. *Psychology for Teaching*, 2nd ed. (Belmont, California: Wadsworth Publishing Company, Inc., 1972) 148-49.

49. E.L.Thorndike, "Reward and Punishment in Animal Learning," *Comparative Psychology Monographs* 8 (1932, No. 39).

50. LeFrancois 36.

51. Robert R. Sears, Eleanor P. Maccoby, and H. Lewin, *Patterns of Child Rearing* (Evanston, Illinois: Row Peterson, 1957).

52. B.F. Skinner, "How to Teach Animals," *Scientific American* 185 (December, 1951) 26-29.

53. William Starr, *The Suzuki Violinist* (Secaucus, New Jersey: Summy-Birchard, 1976).

54. Suzuki, *Love,* 1.

55. B.F. Skinner, *Beyond Freedom and Dignity* (New York: Macmillan, 1967) 200 ff.

56. Starr 141.

57. Albert Bandura and Richard Walters, *Social Learning and Personality Development* (New York: Holt, Rinehart and Winston, 1963).

58. Albert Bandura, "Social Learning Through Imitation," *Nebraska Symposium on Motivation*, ed. H.R. Jones (Lincoln: University of Nebraska Press, 1962) 211-269.

59. LeFrancois 36.

60. Bandura and Walters.

61. Suzuki, *Bulletin*, 3.

62. *Homecoming*, John Bradshaw, PBS, 1991.

63. Shinichi Suzuki, comment during a discussion of the origin of the Talent Education movement. 17, October, 1977.

64. Suzuki, *Love*, 65.

65. Suzuki, *Love*, 65.

66. Suzuki, *Love*, 66.

67. Suzuki, *Love*, 11.

68. Suzuki, *Love*, 12.

69. John Bradshaw, *Healing the Shame That Binds You*, HCI audio books, 1989.

70. John Bradshaw, *Homecoming* (New York: Bantam Books, 1990) 264.

71. Eugene Herrigel, *Zen in the Art of Archery* (New York: Pantheon, 1953).

72. Starr 139.

73. Starr 139.

74. James Gabarino, "The Place of Children in the World Community," Suzuki Association of the Americas Sixth Conference, Chicago, 3 June 1994.

75. Dorothy Jones, *"Parents as Partners,"* Suzuki Association of the Americas Sixth Conference, Chicago, 5 June 1994.

76. Susan Grilli, *Preschool in the Suzuki Spirit* (Tokyo: Harcourt-Brace Javanovich Japan, 1987) 24.

77. Susan Grilli, *Nurturing Parents as Teachers* (New York: Susan Grilli, 1993) 1.

78. Grilli 1.

79. John Bradshaw, *Creating Love* (New York: Bantam Books, 1992).

80. Paula C. Resch, *Suzuki and the Teaching of Writing: A Surprising Connection* (1984), Viewpoints (ERIC ED 251 181) 2.

81. Resch 2.

82. Resch 2.

83. Resch 4.

84. Elizabeth Jones Cherwick, "Preliminary Bibliography of Psychological and Educational Research Involving or Mentioning the Suzuki Method," (University of Alberta, 1994) 9.

85. Cherwick 1-4.

BIBLIOGRAPHY

Bandura, Albert. *Principles of Behavior Modification.* New York: Holt, Rinehart and Winston, 1969.

- - - "Social Learning Through Imitation." *Nebraska Symposium on Motivation* ed. H.R. Jones. Lincoln: University of Nebraska Press, 1962.

Bandura, Albert, and Richard Walters. *Social Learning and Personality Development.* New York: Holt, Rinehart and Winston, 1963.

Bradshaw, John. *Creating Love.* New York: Bantam Books, 1992.

- - - *Healing the Shame that Binds You.* Houston: Bradshaw cassette, 1989.

- - - *Homecoming.* New York: Bantam Books, 1990.

- - - *Homecoming.* Houston: Bradshaw Cassette, 1991.

Cherwick, Elizabeth Jones. "Preliminary Bibliography of Psychological and Educational Research Involving or Mentioning the Suzuki Method." University of Alberta. 1994.

Cook, Clifford. *Suzuki Education in Action.* Jericho: Exposition, 1970.

Dobson, James. *Dare to Discipline.* Wheaton: Tyndale, 1970

"Fiddling Legions." *Newsweek.* 25 March 1964: 73.

151

Gabarino, James. "The Place of Children in the World Community." Suzuki Association of the Americas Sixth Conference. Chicago, 3 June 1994.

Grilli, Susan. *Nurturing Parents as Teachers.* New York: Susan Grilli, 1993.

- - - *Preschool in the Suzuki Spirit.* Tokyo: Harcourt-Brace Jovanovich, Japan, 1987.

Grilli, Susan, and Dorothy Jones. *Grilli and Jones Consultants in Early Education.* New York and London, Canada: Grilli and Jones, 1994.

Herrigel, Eugene. *Zen in the Art of Archery.* New York: Pantheon, 1953.

Jones, Dorothy. *Children's Talent Education Center.* London, Canada: CTEC, 1994.

- - - "Parents as Partners." Suzuki Association of the Americas Sixth Conference. Chicago, 5 June 1994.

LeFrancois, Guy R. *Psychology for Teaching.* 2nd ed. Belmont: Wadsworth Publishing Company, 1972.

Mills, Elizabeth, and Sr. Therese Cecile Murphy, eds. *The Suzuki Concept.* Berkeley: Diablo Press, Inc. 1973.

Pavlov, I.P. *Conditioned Reflexes.* London: Oxford University Press, 1927.

Resch, Paula C. "Suzuki and the Teaching of Writing: A Surprising Connection" (1984). ERIC ED 251- 181.

Sears, Robert R., Maccoby, Eleanor P., and Lewin, H. *Patterns of Child Rearing.* , Evanston: Row, Peterson, 1957.

Skinner, B.F. *Beyond Freedom and Dignity.* New York: Macmillan, 1967.

- - - "How to Teach Animals." *Scientific American.* December, 1951: 26-29.

- - - *Science and Human Behavior.* New York: Macmillan, 1952.

- - - *Verbal Behavior.* New York: Appleton-Century-Craft, 1957.

Starr, William. *The Suzuki Violinist.* Secaucus, New Jersey: Summy-Birchard, 1976.

Suzuki, Daisetz. *The Essentials of Zen Buddhism.* Ed. Bernard Phillips. New York: E.P. Dutton, 1962.

Suzuki, Shinichi. *Bulletin from the Second International Conference on Talent Education.* Matsumoto: Talent Education Institute, 1977.

- - - *Law of Ability and the "Mother Tongue Method" of Education.* Matsumoto, Japan: Talent Education Institute, 1973.

- - - *Nurtured by Love.* 2nd ed. Athens: Senzay, 1983.

- - - Suzuki *Cello School.* Secaucus, New Jersy: Summy-Birchard, 1980.

- - - Suzuki *Piano School.* Secaucus, New Jersey: Summy-Birchard, 1978.

- - - Suzuki *Viola School.* Secaucus, New Jersey: Summy-Birchard, 1981.

- - - Suzuki *Violin School.* Secaucus, New Jersey: Summy-Birchard, 1978.

Suzuki, Shunugu. *Zen Mind, Beginners Mind.* Tokyo: Weatherhill, 1970.

Thorndike, E.L. "Reward and Punishment in Animal Learning." *Comparative Psychology Monographs.* 1932, 8, No. 39.

- - - *Selected Writings From a Connectist's Psychology.* New York: Appleton-Century-Crafts, 1949.

Watson, J.B. *Behaviorism.* Chicago: The University of Chicago Press, 1930.

Yampolsky, Philip B, ed. *The Zen Master Hakuin.* New York: Columbia University Press, 1971.

Dr. Carolyn M. Barrett with her granddaughter Mariam

About the Author

Dr. Carolyn M. Barrett, Director of the Suzuki Music Studio in Reston, Virginia, U.S.A., also founded Suzuki Studios in Lagos, Nigeria and Seoul, Korea. The Seoul studio trained sixty students weekly, and instructed British, Korean, and American educators in using the Suzuki approach in teaching stringed instruments, especially violin. The Seoul studio was directly supervised by Dr. Suzuki; students sent tapes to him for graduation certification. Dr. Barrett traveled three times to Matsumoto, Japan to study with Dr. Shinichi Suzuki. Dr. Barrett gives group and individual instruction in violin, viola, cello, and piano using both traditional and Suzuki educational strategies. She has thirty years teaching experience. The Reston studio presents recitals and gives performance in the Washington, D.C. metropolitan area. Students have concertized at the White House and participated in concerts at Wolf Trap, Constitution Hall, and the Kennedy Center.

As a performer, Dr. Barrett has been a choral and instrumental conductor, violinist, pianist, and violist. She was a violinist with the Spokane Symphony Orchestra, Twenty-First Century, a piano trio; Trio Allegro, Pro Musica Lagos and the Yongsan Chamber Music Society. She is a piano accompanist for Suzuki recitals and accompanied performances and classes at the Cassarno Ballet Studios in Portland and Lake Oswego, Oregon. Dr. Barrett teaches advanced English composition at George Mason University in Fairfax, Virginia.